Questioning Death

A true story of loss, wonder and liberating answers

Copyright © 2006
by G. G. Albert

Questioning Death
by G. G. Albert

Printed in the United States of America

ISBN 1-60034-313-9

All rights reserved solely by the author. The author guarantees all contents are original and do not infringe upon the legal rights of any other person or work. No part of this book may be reproduced in any form without the permission of the author. The views expressed in this book are not necessarily those of the publisher.

Unless otherwise indicated, Bible quotations are taken from the Authorized King James Version.

www.xulonpress.com

Contents

1. Is Grandpa In Heaven? 11
2. Did God Take My Brother? 17
3. Do Others Struggle With Death Like I Did? 23
4. Did God Know How I Was Feeling? 29
5. Can I Understand The Bible? 35
6. Did Jesus Explain Death? 41
7. Why All the Confusion? 49
8. Aren't Human Souls Immortal? 57
9. What About the Spirit? 65
10. When Does A Person Go To Heaven? 71
11. Does It Really Matter What I Believe? 77
12. What About Near Death Experiences? 83
13. Can Visitations Be Explained? 89
14. Can We Communicate With The Dead? 97
15. Don't Some Text Teach An Immediate Reward? 107
16. What About the Promise to The Thief? 115
17. Would A Loving God Torment People Forever? 121
18. When Will The Church Be Raptured? 131
19. Wouldn't A God of Love Save Everyone? 141
20. Is God Really Like A Loving Father? 149

21. Will Simply Believing In Jesus Get Me
    Into Heaven?... 157
22. How Does All of This Information Fit Together?..... 165
23. When Will the World End?....................................... 177
24. What Must I Do To Be Saved?................................. 183

In Dedication

This book is dedicated in memory of my brother Bobby.
I also want to thank my parents,
my surviving brother, my sister and my wife.
All of you have stuck by me in good times and in bad.
I love you.

Preface

For a very long time I had a problem with God. It wasn't anything personal, in fact, it couldn't be. You see, I had no idea who or what He was. Sure, I had to admit that there must have been some intelligence involved in the making of a world so beautiful and balanced. But I just didn't feel any connection to an eternal being when I needed it most.

Of all the reasons why I had difficulty believing in a loving God, what I had heard about those who have died brought me the most anxiety. This didn't really hit me hard until the death of my brother. Did God choose to take him from his family because He loved him more than we did? And if so, could my brother now see us on earth, struggling to make sense of it all? What if he didn't make it to heaven for some reason. Would he be with all the rest of those people who would supposedly burn in hell forever and ever?

Many in our world have questions about death. Because of this we seek answers. However, death is not something that humans are comfortable talking about. Maybe our pride prevents us from revealing to anyone else that we really have no clue what happens at death. Maybe it just hurts so much to talk about those we have lost that we simply try not to think about it. But it doesn't go away. No, it's still there. And it still hurts.

Everyone has a story. And I have chosen to share mine. You will learn that my life has not always been a smooth ride. Quite frankly, I have made many mistakes and had many struggles just like everyone else, some of which have been recorded in this book. However, even though it was often very difficult to recall the tough times and re-live the emotions once again, I am going to take you along on this journey with me anyway. Why? Because through it all, I have learned some things that just might help someone else.

Have you ever found yourself questioning death? Then I believe this book is for you.

The Author

Chapter 1

Is Grandpa In Heaven?

*M*y grandfather was just sixty-three when he had his heart attack and it was a surprise to all. When we had gotten the call the day before, dad was told the attack was a pretty bad one so mom and dad decided they had better make the trip, just in case. I remember my dad pulling into the driveway at the farm where mom was raised. It was always the first place we would stop when getting into town and when we saw my mom's parents coming out to greet us we knew something was wrong. Dad for sure must have known right away as he got out of the car with a look on his face as if he feared the worst. Mom told us to stay in for a minute while they talked. We didn't understand at the time but obeyed. After some words and hugs dad continued into the house. Mom knew we were too late. "Grandpa must have died," she whispered.

After getting out of the car there were more hugs and tears and then us kids were asked to stay outside and play for a while. Dad would spend quite a bit of time in the bedroom by himself while mom and grandma made plans for us. Because we had not expected to stay for more than a day or so, we didn't come prepared for a funeral. Therefore, mom would have to drive the two and one half hours back home to get our good clothes and we would stay at the farm for the next couple of days. We were told dad would go into town to be with our other grandma while mom was away.

I don't remember very much about the next few days but I do know things were happening very fast. I also knew that from now on, things would be different. Even though I was only six, I realized this would be the last time I would see my grandpa's face before they would put him in the ground. Six years old is much too young to have to experience a loved one's death. But is there ever a good age when we can be comfortable with the idea that we may never see a loved one again? I think not. Death can be a very difficult thing to deal with for anyone, especially when you don't know what happens next. For me, all I knew at that time was that I was very sad. And so was daddy.

We were not regular church goers but did make some appearances on special occasions and holidays. Our mixed, Lutheran/Catholic family never really discussed the deep things of religion. Sure, we were taught to believe in God, and like most families, we prayed before meals and before bed. But for me, a kid, believing in God was nothing more than acknowledging something out there, maybe out of fear, fear of not going to heaven when I died. Of course, when you believe in heaven you have to believe in the other place too. Well, at least that's what we were taught.

As we walked into the funeral home I truly didn't know what to expect. Being so young, this would be my first time I would ever see someone who was, well, dead. I had listened to all the talk, the mysterious talk that goes with that type of situation but didn't really know anything. Terms like, he passed on, or, he passed away were new to me. Maybe by going through this experience I would learn where he went.

Questioning Death

During that first funeral I wondered why people were crying so much. After all, the minister spoke of grandpa being in heaven and there was all of those flowers. But there were many tears, and the tissues, and the hugs. If grandpa was really going to heaven why did everyone seem so sad? Were they sad because they missed him already? Or, were they sad because they had doubts about ever seeing him again? Maybe they weren't quite sure where he was going, if anywhere.

Before the ceremony, I remember my dad picking me up to see grandpa laying there in the casket. I saw that grandpa was dressed up and appeared to be sleeping. He was a fairly large man of about six feet, three inches tall with a bald head and wire-rim glasses. Grandpa had only one arm as he had lost the other in an accident at one of the many jobs he had undertaken over the years. But you couldn't tell he was missing an arm by the way they had positioned him. He was surrounded by white satin cloth and looked relatively comfortable. If he was really going to heaven, he was sure dressed up nice.

What I remember most about grandpa was his gentle demeanor and his strong hand and arm. I remember him helping me up as I would attempt to climb up on his lap and snap his suspenders as we both would laugh. I also remember him singing *Oh, Christmas Tree* in German with a deep strong voice. I do not have very many memories of grandpa but I was told later that he had a fairly hard life. If that were the case I sure couldn't tell it when we would visit. He seemed pretty kind and happy to me, but maybe he just acted that way around his grandkids. People sometimes do that you know. But I will remember the little things the most, like the suspenders and the song. I only wish I could have spent more time with him. Sixty-three just seems too young to die.

Questioning Death

I thought we were going to the funeral to say goodbye. But as the minister spoke about seeing him again, it gave everyone hope. Maybe I would know more as I got older but it was all mysterious to me at the time. How did the minister know we would see him again? What if it turns out that I am not a good enough person to go to heaven? I cannot say for sure that I thought about these things at the time. It's not as though young kids think that deep about anything. But the words I heard along with the images and emotions were etched in my mind and would continue to enter my thoughts time and time again.

As I got older, it wouldn't take much to bring me back to grandpa's funeral. Whether I saw something on television, or maybe in a movie, or even in the newspaper, whenever someone died, I wondered. Some die young, some old. Some die tragically, some quietly. I hate to say it but at the time, I believed that some people deserved to die. And yet others probably didn't deserve to die at all. Whatever the reason for it, whether death was just a natural part of life or not, I would be increasingly aware of it's reality as the years passed. From what I could see through my six year old eyes and onward, death was a bad thing. Maybe it was a happy time for those who experienced it, but for those left behind, it was hard to see that anyone could be happy about losing a loved one.

Grandpa's funeral was the first of many in my life. And, as much as I tried to make sense of it all, I couldn't. With the whole gamut of rituals, graveyards and crosses, incense and chants, robes, candles and talk of ashes and dust, I wondered what it all meant. Did any of these preachers really know what happened to those who had passed away? As I would see statues of Jesus on crosses illuminated by candlelight within a dark atmosphere and strange organ music, it was hard to understand how any of these things were really bringing comfort to anyone.

Maybe it was just me, but I would become more and more confused as time passed. As much as I wanted to believe death was a good thing, I could not see the good in it at all. Even though I was getting older and should've had more knowledge about this issue, my view of death had not changed much from the time I was six. No matter how I looked at it, when I would take everything surrounding death into consideration, death was like a bad dream, a great mystery, not something that was a part of life, but simply the end of it. And I really missed not seeing my grandpa.

Why are people given life just to have it taken away, often in a relatively short time? How could this be part of a great master plan from a God who is supposed to love everybody? I sure couldn't find the love in losing someone close to me. And I know for certain that my mom and dad struggled as well. I often wondered why my dad spent so much time in his bedroom alone as we were growing up. But as time passed and I watched him suffer, not only through grandpa's death, but his brother's, I began to understand. To this day I still feel sorry for what my dad had to go through, or should I say, what he is still going through. And maybe I even felt sorry for myself. Yes, I had lost a grandpa and an uncle, but even more than that, I lost my dad. I lost him for many days, and weeks, and even more as he had to deal with these losses and whatever went along with them. There is just this feeling of unfairness attached to death that is hard to shake no matter how much time passes.

To whatever degree a person is affected by death, one thing is for sure, everyone is. I doesn't matter who or where you are, or even if a person is old enough to know what is going on, all of us have experienced the impact of this strange part of life. Some may be able to handle death easier than others, or maybe they just hide it better. But for some reason, I am one of those types who didn't handle it well. And I believe there is at least one more person who wonders about death like I do. Yes, maybe there are many. In fact, there might even be thousands, or millions who are hung up on the real meaning of life, and death.

Maybe you are one of the many that have questions about death. If you are, I'm glad. Why would I be glad about that? Well, the simple fact that you picked up this little book tells me that I am not alone in this quest for answers. Yes, I guess that means I am not crazy or anything like that. It means that I am not the only one who has felt the deep sadness, the denial, the regret, the loneliness, the anger, and the helplessness that is experienced by those who have lost loved ones.

Chapter 2

Did God Take My Brother?

"Oh, he's so young." This was the most common response when friends and relatives heard about my brother. It was as if they already knew the fact that when someone had cancer, especially brain cancer, it was a sure death sentence. I'm sure twenty-two seems young to those in their forties and above. But the thing that struck me the most about the repeated response was the supposed finality of it all.

As the middle brother, just three years older than Bobby, I just didn't want to spend time thinking about losing him. Instead, my first reaction was one of disbelief and then denial. Right away I started researching and making phone calls attempting to find a way, any way, to beat this thing. I don't know if it was because we were the two middle kids with an older brother and younger sister, or because we were buddies with a lot of the same interests, but I felt obligated to find a cure. Death was simply not an option.

Even though almost twenty years and many funerals had come and gone since grandpa died, I was still basically in the dark with regard to death. Sure, it was getting a little easier to take with all the talk of no more pain and the departed being in a better place, but still there was that confusion. Who really knew for sure where my young brother would go if he did lose this battle?

I can still remember that day of the surgery when the doctor was to come and tell us how everything went. In this small waiting room where the family all sat quietly, we waited, and waited. We were not a family who regularly participated in open prayer but I'm a certain that each of us silently offered one during that time that seemed like forever.

When the doctor came in it was like one of those good news, bad news situations that we always hear about. At least that's the way the doctor tried to paint the scene. "The surgery went well," he said, "we removed a grapefruit-sized tumor from Robert's brain and he's doing fine." Mom was quick to ask the questions from there. "So he's okay?" "Unfortunately, we only were able to get about ninety-five percent of the tumor and we are hoping that with chemo and radiation therapy we can reduce the tumor even more," the doctor answered. "So, it is cancer?" Mom asked with tears streaming down all of our faces. "I'm sorry. We will wait for the biopsy to come back but I have done many surgeries like this and I am pretty certain the tumor was cancerous." It was my turn to jump in. "So with radiation and chemo he will be fine right?" The doctor hesitated, "I'm sorry but all the chemo and radiation can do is hopefully slow the re-growth of the tumor." "How about going back in?" "The nature of this type of tumor is such that is wraps itself around the good tissue and it has actually penetrated very sensitive areas of the brain that's why we couldn't get it all." "How long does he have then?" Dad asked. "Six months to a year at best. We want to start the treatments right away once we get the tests back and are sure of the type." "So there is still a chance that it's not cancerous?" Dad said. "I'm sorry but I don't think that's possible. We are quite certain."

After thanking the doctor for all he did, the nurse allowed us to stay in the private room for a time of mourning while we waited to see Bobby. Then later, one by one we went in to see him, keeping what we had just heard to ourselves. Because he was still groggy from the anesthesia he probably wouldn't have understood anyway. At least that's what I thought. But when we went into the room he asked almost immediately. "How bad is it?" Mom told him that they took out a large tumor and they were going to give him treatments to help him. "Is it cancer?" "Yes," she said, "they're pretty sure it is but the doctor is going to wait for the tests to come back to be certain."

Bobby was silent as if he knew. And as I held his hand and told him I would see him later I had a hard time holding back the tears. From that moment on, and still through today, I wonder if it was harder on us than it was on him. Now, I'm sure of it. Bobby seemed to handle things very well, as if he was sparing us. Even after he knew everything the doctor told us, he didn't seem to take it as hard as we did.

During the next few weeks of recovery at home my brother was trying his best to get on with his life. We even had a party for him that we had been planning even prior to his surgery. You see Bobby was a very talented young person and recently returned from a year in South America where he worked as a crew leader at a construction site. Unfortunately, even though he had saved a lot of money and had made plans for continuing his career in the States, the headaches started just a few weeks before his return. Sometimes you just have bad luck I guess.

As the next few weeks passed and word got around about his illness, some friends came to visit, but many that we thought would come calling, didn't. I remember one unlikely friend, Craig, who we had played softball with, came by one day almost as soon as he heard. Craig had been going through some troubles of his own but for whatever reason, was taking Bobby's illness very hard. In fact, his passion and concern was almost overwhelming. We had a hard time understanding why Craig was so concerned about Bobby as they weren't really that close. Although reluctant, we went along with whatever Craig had in mind, at least for a few days.

The odd thing about this situation was that once people found out that Craig was coming over to see Bobby, we received calls from some of his friends explaining that he was experiencing some medical problems and they feared he had a chemical imbalance. However, we didn't see any reason to keep Craig from coming over. He seemed sincere enough.

One example of Bobby's strength regarding his fate happened during the stressful time of beginning treatments. Our friend Craig came over one day just as we had arrived back home after radiation treatments determined to take Bobby to his church. He was adamant about having us talk to his pastor and Bobby agreed. Of course, I went along as well. It appeared Craig had a tremendous burden concerning my brother's eternal destiny and we decided it wouldn't hurt to go along. You never know, maybe he knew something we didn't. At least, that's what we thought at the time.

I do not recall that Presbyterian pastor's name but I do recall that he was just as surprised about our visit as I was. Apparently this was totally unplanned and that pastor seemed to be at least a little shocked at Craig's request for council and prayer. However, with a quiet and caring demeanor, this minister counseled with the three of us. He asked Bobby if he believed in God and if he had ever accepted Jesus as his Savior. He calmly told the pastor that he did in fact believe in God. After some other questions and a scripture reading, the pastor asked what Bobby thought about having cancer. I will never forget the answer as it was both assuring and perplexing at the same time. I could not argue with his logic and was amazed by his calmness as he told the pastor that

Questioning Death

he believed the reason why he was stricken with this disease was that God must have had another job for him to do. He made it sound so simple and he seemed so sure. Here I was breaking down along with Craig while my mind was refusing to admit the awful possibility that he was dying. On top of that, the idea that God was possibly taking him from us must have contributed to my emotions. But again, just like the day in the hospital, Bobby was as calm as could be.

The pastor seemed as surprised as anyone at Bobby's response. And, it probably made his job relatively easy knowing that this young man was seemingly at peace with his situation. After the pastor closed with a prayer that God would have mercy upon Bobby while also asking for strength for the days ahead, we thanked the kind man and made our way outside without a word.

Even though my brother appeared to be at peace, I was not. Sure, I was happy for him. And maybe it was all just a simple as he believed it was. Maybe God did have a plan for him. But I still couldn't help feeling sorry for myself and angry as well. Yes, I was angry with God. There were many reasons for feeling the way I did. Maybe it was partly because I had not been the best of brothers, or the best of people as far as that goes. Whether God was punishing my brother, or me, or even my family, I did not know. Why would God allow this young man to go through something like this? If he had a job for him to do as Bobby believed, why couldn't he just take him quickly?

During the next few months as the family was holding out hope that Bobby would make it, his actions showed that he knew his life was nearing the end. My brother did things that he had never done before simply because he knew he was not going have a full life. He told me that he had never had his own dog, so he got Natasha, a Siberian husky pup. He had never owned a motorcycle, so he purchased one of them also. Then he bought himself a Chevy Blazer and said he had never been to Florida, so we took a trip down there between his treatments. He was sick most of the time but at least he was able to say that he'd been there. Fortunately, Bobby had managed to save quite a little bit of money while working hard the last few years which allowed him to do what he did, otherwise none of those things would have been possible. Some people are not so lucky. Well, maybe lucky is not the right term.

Fortunately, Bobby was able to garner the strength to stand in our older brother, Denny's wedding in April of that year, but after that, he struggled to keep his spirits up. For the next few months he sold many possessions and became a Big Brother. This was because, as he put it, "I know I may never get a chance to get married and be a dad so maybe I can help some kid now." Bobby was a good looking young man with a big heart. He did not deserve to die. When the doctor told us he had six months to a year to live I couldn't believe it. Even after his cancer had spread to his spine and brain stem, and after the most stressful time in our family's life, it was still hard believing it was happening. But it did. In September of that year my little brother was gone at the age of twenty-three. Did God really take him because he had a job for him to do? Is that how God works?

Chapter 3

Do Others Struggle With Death Like I Did?

I took the rest of the day off after the service and luncheon that followed and simply went home to be alone. Karen and I would be married in a little more than two weeks. And, as much as we were hoping Bobby could hang on to stand in the wedding as our best man, it wasn't meant to be. Maybe he would be watching, at least that's what I hoped. If that was not possible I knew that he would be there in spirit and in the hearts of everyone. Even though postponing the wedding was discussed, we knew that a wedding, even a bitter-sweet one, was better than continuing to dwell on our sorrow. Life goes on as they say and we knew that Bobby probably would have wanted all of us to move forward with our lives.

Gazing out of the sliding glass door of the A-frame house that Karen and I would soon call home, I could not help but to wonder what was next for my little brother. While thinking about the many good times we had together and also the bad times, it seemed like the bad times ruled. This was most likely due to the fact that I wasn't always a very good brother. Realizing just how selfish of a person I had been, I wished it were possible to go back and undo some of the things I had done. Maybe if I had been a better brother, Bobby would still be alive today.

With tears and a few smiles I thought of him and talked with him not knowing whether he could hear me or not. But I just sat there numb, gazing out the window while wiping an occasional tear from my eye. I hoped for any sign that would let me know that he heard me and that everything would be alright. Maybe I was being selfish but I have to say I felt so alone, and guilty.

I had heard of strange things happening to others who had lost loved ones and I was hoping for the same: A visitation, a voice or some other strange occurrence, anything to help me feel that Bobby was okay. Even though he seemed to be confident in a next level of life until the end, I wasn't quite as stable about the whole thing as he was.

For me to even think that I had some sort of great connection to the other side would have been quite a stretch. In fact, I never did little more than make an occasional appearance at church, any church. Sure, I still believed, at least sort of, but I also have to admit that I was angry with God. Because of this, you can probably guess that I did not have a lot of confidence in whoever or whatever was out there. Again I attempted to talk to Bobby himself as if that would somehow help me get through this time. I had heard people say that God is in all of us and, just maybe, I could get some kind of direct line. But I didn't hear or feel a thing.

Kicking my feet up on the couch and propping a pillow under my head I decided to attempt a nap. But to my surprise I noticed a small group of sparrows gathering in the beautiful little birch tree just off the deck. As I watched the birds I wondered if this just might be a repeat of what Karen had experienced just after her grandfather died. Could these be God's little messengers letting me know that Bobby was safe?

Questioning Death

As more and more sparrows gathered in the only tree that was clearly within my view, I watched as there was so many that they almost had to battle for space to perch. This had to be a sign. As I watched in amazement I wondered if this was a coincidence or was this in fact the answer I was hoping for. With tears of sadness mixed with tears of joy I accepted this sign. Whether it was from God himself or from Bobby who now had the power to command these little creatures to help and ease my suffering, either way, I would take it.

That event happened on September 29, 1983, and for the next six years Karen and I went through many ups and downs in our marriage and in our lives. I tried to be strong and supportive for my parents, and especially my dad who took Bobby's death very hard. I know mom struggled with losing her youngest son as well but being raised in a strong and proud Catholic family she very seldom displayed her deep sadness. If you were to ask her, she would tell you that coping with Bobby's death was easier than having to watch him waste away for the ten months while he was losing the battle. Even though you miss them so much, many find comfort in the simple fact that their loved ones are no longer suffering.

I often thought mom knew something more about death than the rest of us. Maybe she had just learned to cope with death over the years. Whatever the reason for her apparent peace with it all, mom definitely was a source of continued strength for the family. My older brother and younger sister seemed to handle things pretty well also. They both kept busy with life in general and didn't talk about it much. They were probably also relieved that Bobby was no longer suffering as well. And I also think they believed that he was now in a better place. Maybe they were struggling like I was but were too proud to let anyone know about it. And I also wondered if they questioned the meaning of it all, and if they had made any attempts to talk to Bobby as I had. Because I might have been the only weird one, I never asked. Maybe someday we can discuss it together after I give them a copy of this book.

My dad's struggle was very apparent. He is the type that keeps things pretty much to himself. The problem with that method is that he has difficulty grieving and then moving on. I often thought this was partly due to the fact that he never really had any hobbies or other interests outside of work. Sometimes, this helps to keep your mind off the sad things from the past, at least that's what I have heard.

Unfortunately, from a young age, dad learned to cope with life's problems by isolating himself and by seeking comfort through the use of alcohol and prescription drugs. The reason why I say unfortunately is because I think he would now admit they only cover up the problem and don't actually help you cope at all. I know this because I believe dad and I are a lot alike. We are both deep thinkers and we both have a predisposition for substance abuse as a method of coping with life.

I believe my dad is full of love and concern for others but often became incapacitated because of unresolved issues from his past. This episode with Bobby really threw him into a tailspin of bad memories and regret. However, time has helped to heal at least some of the pain. But he still has bouts of depression around the times of Bobby's birthday and also on the anniversary of his death.

My parents and I have not talked about my feelings, thoughts and doubts about the fate of Bobby. And I've never told them about my experience on that day of the funeral. Maybe it's because I didn't want them to know that I was really struggling with the whole scene. Or maybe it was because I wanted them to think I was strong. But probably most of all was that I didn't want them to carry any more burdens.

Everyone copes with life and death differently. Either I am totally weird and different than most, or everyone has the same struggles. Doing my best to follow the example and

Questioning Death

advice of others, I stayed pretty active most of the time. And if keeping busy didn't help to bury the questions still unresolved in my mind then drugs and alcohol would. I guess I sort of followed in dad's footsteps.

Working in the printing business, enjoying music, sports and partying passed for a life at least for a while. But as time brought me into my thirties the real meaning of what my life was supposed to be all about was not only foremost in my mind, but also illusive. The things of the world just did not seem to be filling the void, or hole in my heart. As much as I tried to bury or hide the signs, I was still hurting inside. From the constant questions in my mind about Bobby's death to the struggles with infertility that Karen and I were experiencing, the frequent arguments over drinking and smoking, things were beginning to unravel. I knew that if something didn't change I would not only have lost my brother but also my marriage as well.

Maybe it was what Bobby said about God having a job for him to do that caused me to question everything. If I were to believe the way he did then that would mean that I could be taken at any time. So what's the point in pursuing success in this life?

To be honest I thought that maybe I was a little different, as if I might have some mental illness. Some would have probably wondered what the problem was. With an attractive wife, good job, a nice house, many friends to party with, and no money problems, what would I have to complain about. Quite frankly, they would have been right. I should have been happy when compared to many others with less.

Watching people, old and young, healthy and sick, toiling through life but appearing to be content with what they have, I felt almost ashamed for even being depressed. I even contemplated suicide on more than one occasion but knew that doing something so drastic would just put Karen and my family through more pain. And of course, it would've just crushed dad.

I wondered if other people go through what I did and if they desire to have more than what life on earth has to offer. Do other people feel that some afterlife existence will provide the contentment we seek? If so, what does life on earth mean? Is this some sort of test? Do only the good people go to heaven? Do other people wonder if they would be with their loved ones if they took their own lives? Or, do they think people go to hell because killing themselves would be considered a sin? And what if there was no heaven at all? What then?

Chapter 4

Did God Know How I Was Feeling?

Whether God could see that I was desperate for answers, or not, I just didn't know it at the time. In fact, I hate to admit it but I wasn't even sure there was a God. And if there was, I didn't really know if I wanted to learn more about him or not. However, something inside me really wanted, and needed to have hope. I needed faith in something to keep going. I needed some meaning for my life. And if there really was a God, then he, if anyone, should be able to lead me to the truth. My gut told me that my brother just had to be somewhere.

As I mentioned earlier I was raised in a typical, mixed-faith American family where my mother was brought up Catholic and my father was raised Lutheran. We attended church sometimes but not on a regular basis. When we did attend, it was the Lutheran church that my parents chose but to tell you the truth, neither I, nor the rest of the kids got much out of it as far as I could tell. When visiting our relatives up north we would occasionally visit the Catholic Church. But there again, it would only be because of some holiday, or funeral. Still, I did not know very much about either denomination. What I did know was that there were definitely differences. My view was that the Catholic Church was more ritualistic in nature while the Lutherans were much more grace oriented. Because I was not deeply grounded in either, and for the reason of pleasing my future wife, I agreed to begin attending the Methodist church. This was of course the church we were eventually married in,

For the next few years after our marriage we maintained a semi-regular attendance record while routinely sitting with my in-laws. However, the simple attendance didn't really do much for giving me any more of a spiritual understanding than I had prior to that time. I truly realize that I was not putting much into learning about the Bible on my own and I'd have to say that for the most part, I was simply going through the motions. Therefore, I definitely was no further ahead in understanding the meaning of life, or death.

One thing that did help through those years of attending the Methodist church was that I began believing in God once again. This was a major breakthrough for me but I still wasn't really getting it. I could not blame my parents or the church for my questions concerning faith. No, I would have to take responsibility for my own ignorance. However, the world, especially the confusion and division in the religious world, sure didn't help.

Sometimes it seemed that there were as many beliefs and opinions about critical issues as there were denominations. Although it probably sounds strange, I really did want to know God better while also becoming disgusted with the whole thing at the same time. I knew the only place my party lifestyle would lead would be a temporary medicated state, or worse, and I really did want more. The problem was that I didn't know where to get it.

Unfulfilled and confused I continued going through the motions. It had been six years since Bobby died and

Questioning Death

I wasn't fulfilled. I had given religion what I thought was a reasonable shot but still had those questions. Having a clouded mind due to my party life didn't help either. So I pulled back. I had convinced myself that I gave it a good effort but could no longer see the point in pursuing religion any further. To be honest my life seemed to be no better, or worse, whether I attended church or not. In fact, I actually felt less guilty about my potentially harmful habits if I didn't attend at all. Even though I wouldn't have admitted it at the time, I needed help.

As time went on, and as I traveled to and fro during the day and stared at the ceiling at night, I wondered about everything from the meaning of life to what happens at death. Did I really need faith in my life? Or, did I already have enough faith to get me through? From what I could tell, most everybody else that I knew claimed to have some affiliation with a church. So maybe I was just fine. But how was I to really know for sure? And how would I ever really be sure that Bobby was ready? Maybe faith was all about attitude. Maybe if you just believe in something hard enough it would be true. If this were actually the case then perhaps Bobby would be in heaven simply because he believed that he would be.

I guess this is why I fought with all of this so much. It bothered me that there was not just some place I could go, or a person I could talk to for answers. And I guess I was still at least a little angry with God. Why did this have to be such a mystery? If God was a God of love then how could he allow people like me to agonize over what should be simple stuff? Is my wanting to know our purpose on this earth too much to ask? And how about what happens to a person when they die, does it really have to be a big mystery?

Looking back at my thoughts and feelings during that period it would not have been out of the question to begin considering evolution as the most logical explanation for our existence. At least there was some apparent science behind it's theory. After all, it was taught in schools in the same way it is today! Could it be that this is done because other people have the same questions about life? Do people believe and teach evolution as an option for the reason for our existence because they really don't know if there is a God?

Dear friend, if you are reading this book today because you are frustrated with life in general, don't give up. If you are disillusioned with religion, hang in there. If you have lost a loved one and the loss has turned your life upside down, keep reading. God is watching. I didn't realize it then but I know now that God was watching me the whole time. Maybe it doesn't seem like it at times but He is there and He is watching you too. He wants you to know the truth about death. And as you continue reading you will see why I can make these statements with confidence.

Yes, God must have been watching. Not only that, but He must have been orchestrating things so that I would find the answers to my questions. I truly believe now He knew that I was desperate for answers, and that there was so much more to learn before I would understand. However, He was not about to force me into anything against my will.

I believe that revealing the truth about these things to all people is in God's divine plan. For this to happen our prideful hearts need to be softened and our minds cannot be cluttered with all of our pre-conceived ideas. Otherwise, we will just become more confused. How do I know? I know it because this is what happened to me. But something inside me, or maybe outside of me, was fighting it all the way. And even when God was presenting an opportunity for me to know more about Him, I almost missed it.

God presents opportunities. And, through using people who believe in Him; those that were lead by His spirit, He will orchestrate those opportunities even though the devil may work to prevent us from seeing them. Fortunately for me, and because of my wife, we didn't miss this one. Because someone cared, we received a card in our mailbox offering free Bible studies. When Karen asked if I was interested in studying the Bible, my response was a resounding no thanks! That may surprise you after all I have shared but understand I was pretty much disgusted with religion at that point. I had gone through the motions and was resigned to the idea that it might be better if I just kept things to myself. And remember, something was holding me back, maybe pride, maybe the devil.

Although I was very curious I also felt it would be just more of the same, just more feel-good, superficial ideas would not give the answers I needed. Truly, my fear was committing to something that would only turn out to be a disappointment in the end. As much as Karen was persistent in asking me about participating, I held my ground. I told her to go ahead and send the card in if she wanted but I would pass. But I also gave in a little by telling her that if the studies turned out to be something really special, then I might reconsider.

Even though those words came from my mouth, something inside was moving me to consider at least giving it a try. I knew that with the struggles we had been through, if nothing else, just maybe it would make my wife happy if I agreed. Somewhat reluctantly, I told Karen that if she began the first study and thought it would be worth my time, then I would attend the studies with her. She was more than willing to honor my wishes. I really didn't know if I would ever get to the studies when I agreed. But in the back of mind I really hoped that maybe, just maybe, this would be just what I needed.

Was it God's will that my brother died? Was it God's will that we were sent an invitation to study the Bible? When we are in a sustained period of grief it's natural to question everything. We can doubt that God is really in control and wonder who is really pulling the strings, especially when things aren't going well. If there was a God, would he really be concerned about someone like me who hardly acknowledged Him? Sometimes it's hard not to believe in a supreme being when we look all around at the amazing beauty and balance in the universe. But it was difficult for me to believe in that same Supreme Being having any personal interest in my life. If He did, then why would He allow my brother to die so young?

A few weeks after sending the card in for the studies, Karen received a visit from two older people. I was not home at the time and was a little concerned about that once I heard but the idea that it was a man and a woman together eased my mind somewhat.

Karen wasn't the least bit put off by the surprised visit and actually had a short and pleasant study with the couple that night. Well, you probably know what happened next. That's right, a Bible study was set up for the next Tuesday and of course, they all thought it would be great if I could be there. Oh, wouldn't that be just wonderful. Somehow, I wasn't all that thrilled.

Chapter 5

Can I Understand the Bible?

The night of the next meeting brought many surprises, not the least of which was the fact that only one of the people showed up. In addition, the one who came over was the older gentlemen who I was not very impressed with. I am normally not judgmental about people especially at first sight but I thought to myself that there was no way this guy was going to get me interested in Bible studies. But I found Pastor Paul to be a nice man, well dressed but tired looking. Actually I thought he was quite an interesting character and we tried to make him feel comfortable as we got acquainted. I had this feeling that I could be doing something else but stayed with it. My thinking was that if I could just make it through this first night, then I could tell Karen this wasn't for me. I was not mean to the old guy at all, in fact, I always have thought of myself as someone who could make friends easily. Although a little suspicious, I did make every effort to give the man a chance.

As I look back at that first night I realize that I may have had help with prejudging this man. I know now that when the devil has you he is not willing to let go. I had heard that God was not willing that anyone would perish and that Satan was like a roaring lion seeking who he may devour. Quotes like this never hit me before like they did that night as this may have been the first time I actually experienced any type of spiritual battle going on in my mind. It wasn't like me to be so uneasy, especially around older folks, so I knew something was happening.

Although I was not initially impressed with this ordinary looking man, I was, however, moved by the pureness and apparent sincerity of the prayer that he opened the study with. Never before had I heard such a sweet and tender request to God for guidance. It made me think of a young child asking a loving Father for a band-aid to cover a scraped knee. The humility that was displayed touched my heart and would open my mind to more of what this old guy had to say.

After spending more time getting acquainted with Paul he proceeded to give us an interesting overview of the Bible. He spoke of the great controversy between God and Satan that began in heaven and would soon culminate into an awful time of trouble here on earth.

Paul told us that from the beginning it was simply pride and jealousy that moved the devil to rebellion against God. He said that the rebellion would not end with Satan alone but a good number of angels, as well as multitudes of people, have been swayed into believing the argument that God was a controlling tyrant. According to Paul, the devil has been able to deceive with the idea that God created beings without free will and that he wanted them to be little more than puppets.

On the flip side of the argument, according to Paul, God created all beings with the free will to make choices for themselves. By simply and clearly showing the ways of darkness and the ways of light, God put forth his plan for a peaceful coexistence among all beings. However, if angels, or man, chose to deny the Creator's way, God is still merciful toward them. And, in that mercy, is not willing to allow them to suffer continually the consequences of their selfish choices. Paul continued to articulate his position that God was, in fact, a loving Father and that His character would be the true focus of the final judgment. As Paul concluded his thought provoking overview he explained to us that from Genesis to Revelation, we see the stories and the consequences of those who have exercised their free will.

I am pretty sure that my wife would agree when I tell you that what this old man had said made a lot of sense. And we appreciated how he clearly laid the groundwork for our study before even opening the book. Although I had very little understanding of spiritual things, I believed that what Paul had shared was probably the feeling of many. Most people truly want to believe that God is love, but there are just so many things we see in this world that make us wonder if this is really the case. Just one look at the daily newspaper or the evening news move many to question if anybody is really in charge.

Up to this point I had not spent any time in meaningful Bible study. This is because I never really thought of the Bible as much more than just a bunch of stories, myths and fables depicting man's struggles in the ancient battle of good versus evil. However, I was about to learn some things that would change my view of the Bible forever. This was because Paul first took the time to show us a very interesting text that I had not heard before.

2 Timothy 3:16 *All scripture is given by inspiration of God, and is profitable for doctrine, for reproof, for correction, for instruction in righteousness:*

As Paul was explaining to us his reason for the overview, my mind jumped ahead to the questions that were weighing heavy on my heart. Was this meeting part of God's will for my life? And, the deeper questions of whether this would lead to helping me to understand the fate of my brother or the many other friends and loved ones who had died. Was it God's will that they died when they did? And where were they now? So badly I wanted to ask Paul these things point blank. But if this was in fact God's way, to let us get the big picture first, then I would go along. Besides, at the time I wasn't too sure Paul was the guy with the answers anyway.

Even though I was becoming more interested in moving ahead with the study, something inside me was telling me to pull the plug on the whole idea right then and there. Then, when Paul said that he was going to start the study in the book of Daniel, instead of a book that was more common like Genesis, Matthew, or Revelation I had real doubts as to where this was going. But the old guy's logic was sound, and looking back, most likely inspired.

Paul told us that the book of Daniel was his favorite book in the entire Bible because it was a prophetic book which foretold world history. As Paul put it, the Prophet Daniel was greatly beloved by God and had actually been given visions in dreams about future events from the time of Babylon right on through our day, to the time of the judgment.

We read and listened intently as the rest of the night would bring the most amazing information I had ever heard. As we read through Daniel together we were especially enlightened to learn how beautifully God had given great visions in dreams to this humble prophet. We learned that Daniel was shown in prophetic fashion the rise and fall of four worldwide empires. Starting from Babylon to the fall of pagan Rome we learned how perfectly Daniel's dreams and interpretations had fit with world history. I was amazed!

Each Tuesday for the next few weeks, Karen and I were both excited to learn of the unquestionable parallels between the Bible and history as we worked through the remaining chapters of the book of Daniel with Paul. And as this elderly guide would say, the Bible is virtually history, or "His Story."

We certainly could understand what he meant. The scriptures opened before us tremendous insights that were not only a review of history but also brought us all the way up to the time of tribulation and judgment.

Paul didn't just read to us either. No, we all took our turn reading and as we did, we were fascinated by the fact that the Bible really does interpret itself. The book of Daniel was our main focus even though we skipped around a little as the Bible says we should do. We learned many things about various characteristics of world empires and whether they were on God's side or the devil's. We learned the true issues surrounding the great battle between good and evil. We even learned that contained in the book of Daniel is the longest time prophecy in the entire Bible which contains proof that Jesus not only came to this earth on time, but he also died on time. And we also learned that God was truly active in the lives of the people of earth.

Was it the will of God that this Bible study came when it did? I think so. Was it God's will that we did not yet get into any deep discussion about the dead? I can honestly say that I believe it was. In hind sight, I probably wasn't ready to know the truth about the dead until I understood all of the issues anyway.

As we studied the Bible, Karen and I both realized that we had known very little in the past. And, even while the studies were going on, the more we learned the more it seemed there was still so much yet to learn. But just when we were thinking all of this stuff could easily overwhelm us, God had other plans. Another surprise was discovered in the mail box. And this surprise would be a great help in leading me to the answers that I was seeking.

Chapter 6

Did Jesus Explain Death?

It had been weeks since we began the studies with Paul and there had been some struggles, mainly internal ones. I was still participating in my party ways during this time and the fact that I was also in Bible studies was not something I discussed with my drinking buddies. Maybe I was too proud or maybe too embarrassed. I may have even felt a little hypocritical. I don't remember for sure what I was thinking at the time but there was definitely a battle going on.

If I knew then what I know now it would have been plain to see that the devil was hanging on while God was giving me the opportunity to break out of the trap. The world had me and the devil knew it. And God, well, He knew it too. But he also knew just how to help me get out in an easy and non-threatening way. Paul was the start of that way, but God also had other people in line to help Karen and I on our journey.

Whether it was just a coincidence, or part of a greater plan, we were pleased to find another surprise in our mailbox when arriving home from work one day. It was an invitation to a seminar that we were very interested in attending. This was not just any seminar, but a Revelation seminar and the timing of it was perfect. We already had the groundwork laid by studying with Paul and now this. The meetings were to be five days a week for four weeks and they would begin in just a few days.

Somewhat reluctant because it seemed like it was a little too much too soon, but knowing that we were really onto something, Karen and I discussed it with our elderly Bible study partner. Paul knew about the meetings and said that his church helped to plan for them. So we agreed to put our Bible studies on hold and began to attend the meetings at the local community center.

Topic by topic I learned more about the Bible than I had ever thought possible about the great battle for the minds of men. Never before had I heard such things and most of them made perfect sense. Although there is so much I could share about the origin of evil, the Bible definition of sin, the nature and mission of Jesus, along with many other wonderful truths, I will attempt to keep this book focused on the subject at hand. However, it is my hope to publish a series of books about finding God's love through other controversial Bible subjects in the coming months.

Much the same way that Paul built a foundation prior to a deeper examination of the Bible, the teacher at the meetings wanted the participants to understand who Jesus was from the onset. In fact, the first few subjects mirrored Paul's overview but with Jesus entwined into every subject.

I believe it was the third night when I realized just how much the devil wanted to deceive man about the true character of God. When I learned about how angry the devil was about the birth of the Savior, and how Revelation twelve told us about his plan was to kill the "seed of the woman" as soon as he was born, it was easy to understand why King Herod gave the orders to kill all the male babies under two years of age in Bethlehem.

Satan's rage toward Jesus makes sense in light of the fact that Jesus was with the Father at the creation, John 1:1-3, and that he was the Word who became flesh and dwelt among us. John 1:14. Also, Jesus is now said to be currently at the right hand of the Father as our advocate, pleading his blood for those who accept him. Hebrew 9:24. And of course he could do this because he paid the penalty for our sins at the cross, Matthew 1:21, and regained the power over death when he rose from the dead. Hebrews 2:14.

Between his birth and death, Jesus was active in performing many miracles like casting out demons, healing people and also raising some from the dead. As I heard these things and began to see that love and compassion he showed, I could not help but to believe God was love. And I could clearly see why Satan has worked so hard to destroy the truth about what Jesus really did for us. Jesus not only died our death, but in doing so he proved that God is, in fact, Love.

Each night as we left the meetings we would be given a sheet of topic notes along with a schedule for the next few nights. When I saw that the subject for the next meeting would be, *Are the Dead Really Dead*, this was the one I had waited for and I just knew we would be there in the front row.

The next night came quickly and I was very nervous. Karen was excited about the subject as well because of the recent loss of her grandfather. We just had to know what these people were going to say about this topic. Did they really know what happens? Does the Bible really give a clear explanation? In just a matter of minutes I would know the truth. At least, that's what I had hoped.

One of the most touching stories in the entire Bible was the one about the death of Lazarus, a good friend of Jesus. I remembered the story from when I was a child but never realized that the key for unlocking the truth about death was revealed within this passage of the Bible.

It was probably for a couple of reasons that I began to accept the story of Lazarus as more than just any story. First was the groundwork that Paul had laid in showing the close relationship between the Bible and history. This foundation not only gave me confidence in the God's word but also a curiosity in what else it had to offer. Secondly, of course it was that this story was about someone's death; something that I had to admit I still knew nothing about.

Please understand at this time I had not made any commitment toward accepting Jesus as my personal Savior. Nor had I even fully recognized my need for salvation. And to be honest, I was still there for basically selfish reasons. I wanted to know what I wanted to know and I had virtually no intention of joining a church. I do recall however, my heart becoming softer and softer with each night as each topic was presented. Frankly, it was hard to learn about Jesus' love and compassion for the weak and poor, and his passion for teaching about the Father's love, without being touched. So when we heard the story about Lazarus I listened intently to learn how Jesus would handle this situation.

It is never wise to base your beliefs upon something someone else tells you so please don't take my word as gospel here. My hope is that you read this account in John chapter eleven for yourself. I am only a human like the rest of you and I am not attempting to do anymore than to paraphrase the passage for the purpose of giving a basic understanding of the Bible account. So again, please read this for yourself!

The story of Lazarus is a touching one when you learn that Mary, Martha and Lazarus were all considered good friends of Jesus. But Jesus was not with them when Lazarus became ill. When he received word that his friend was very sick Jesus was being urged to hurry to his friend's side in order that he could heal Lazarus. Obviously, his followers had witnessed their master perform many miracles. And they must have been pretty sure that Jesus would rush to the bedside of Lazarus. However, after receiving word, Jesus did not immediately go to be with his friend. In fact, the account shows that many were quite perplexed as to why Jesus was not in any hurry.

Some thought that Jesus knew Lazarus would get better and that there was no reason to hurry. But the fact of the matter was that by the time Jesus had finally received word of the condition of his friend, he knew what the message bearers did not.

The account of what happened next may be one of the most important teachings regarding death found anywhere. And keep in mind that it was lived out by Jesus himself, the one person who should know what he's talking about.

When Jesus was asked why he was not in any hurry, he simply said, get this, *"Lazarus sleepeth but I go that I should awake him out of sleep."* John 11:11. As the people wondered about his statement and tried to reason what he meant, one said, *"If he sleepeth he doeth well,"* assuming that rest would be good for Lazarus. Maybe this was why Jesus was not in any hurry to rush to his aid. However, knowing that there was still some confusion among the people, Jesus said plainly, "Lazarus is dead."

What did all this mean? At the time it surely didn't make sense to me until we read the entire story. So let's take a closer look because I do not want any of you to miss this.

Jesus, as plainly as can be was saying that Lazarus was asleep, and dead! Yes, what he was essentially saying was a little confusing to those present but true. Death and sleep, in the biblical sense, are one in the same! But let's stay with the story to get the full context.

The main reason why the people were confused about the two seemingly contradictory statements was probably not the statements themselves, but the fact that he said he would go to "awake him." How was he going to do that if Lazarus was dead? Maybe he wasn't really dead, right?

As we continue deeper into John eleven we learn that upon his arrival in Bethany, Jesus was greeted by Martha, one of the sisters of Lazarus. This woman was in great sorrow and actually comes across in this passage as being a little angry as to why Jesus had not arrived sooner. Jesus tried to console Martha as he stated that her brother would live again. Martha's response was that she knew full well that Lazarus would rise, *"in the resurrection at the last day."* John 11:24. Obviously, Martha knew the truth about when the dead in Christ would rise again. However, her sorrow was not totally quenched by that fact. She missed her brother and Jesus was touched deeply by her sadness.

There were many reasons why Jesus did and said what he had. In fact, earlier in the chapter he told his followers that it was good that he was with them when Lazarus died. Because it happened that they might believe. Why? In his own words, and with many Jews present, he stated, *"I am the resurrection, and the life: he that believeth in me, though he were dead, yet shall he live."* John 11:25.

As Martha went to get her sister Mary from the house and then saw her and many of the Jews that were with them weeping also, the Bible states that Jesus was troubled. But why was Jesus troubled? Was it because they questioned him about his arriving too late? Was it that they did not believe in him? Was it because he had to wait four days because of the common belief that a person was not really considered dead until at least three days? Or, was it because he knew that to bring Lazarus back would mean pulling him out of paradise?

My hope and prayer is that this next foundation stone has the same impact on you that it did on me the night I first heard it. It is powerful! Notice what Jesus said after they rolled the stone away from the tomb. In the midst of doubt and concerns of the body smelling badly because of decomposition, and after a prayer to the Father, Jesus simply said, *"Lazarus, come forth."* John 11:43.

Maybe more important than what Jesus did say, is what he didn't say. He did not say Lazarus come up, or Lazarus come down. No, he simply said, "Lazarus, come forth." Yes, with great anticipation from the crowd of witnesses, many of whom were probably hoping to catch Jesus in the act of claiming to have the power to perform miracles, Jesus came to do what he said he would do, wake his friend out of his state of sleeping the sleep of death.

Taking a little pause here I want to mention another text found in Matthew that also shows death as being a sleep. No, this is not just an isolated incident differing from other text. Actually there are many that describe death as being a sleep and I will give more as we progress. But check this out. It's found in Matthew 27:52 and it tells what happened at the time when Jesus died on the cross.

And the graves were opened: and many bodies of the saints which slept arose.

You see this is not unusual at all. The dead are asleep. And if there was any doubt in my mind about whether Lazarus was actually in heaven at the time when Jesus called his name, the doubt was overcome by a very simple fact. Here is yet another foundation stone for learning the truth about the state of the dead. There is no mention of Lazarus complaining. That's it! You see, if Lazarus, or any one of us for that matter, were to go to heaven upon death, wouldn't we at least say something like, "Hey, what's going on? I was in paradise up there. What are you thinking?" Interesting wouldn't you say? That's what I thought. Sure we can speculate about souls and spirits and all that stuff here, and we will get to those questions later. But for the sake of laying the foundation let's just take this scripture as it reads. Lazarus was sleeping and Jesus woke him out of his sleep.

What great power and compassion Jesus showed that day. What a great reunion was had by the friends and family of Lazarus. Just maybe that was just a little glimpse of what will happen on that last day, at the resurrection.

Did I have other questions? Sure I did. And I got the answers I needed through the meetings and more Bible studies. As we continue through this little book I will share many of those findings with you. But I must say, I will never forget how the story of Lazarus, those words, those thoughts, and that night in general would definitely have a profound impact on my view of Jesus, his love, the Bible, and what happens to people when they die.

Chapter 7

Why All the Confusion?

We still had questions after the meeting about death being like a sleep. Mainly we wondered why so many people believed otherwise. Thinking back to funerals we had attended and all the talk about heaven, and with the things we had heard and read regarding hellfire, I always went along with the crowd and believed the dead were either in one place or the other. This puzzled me.

Was it true that when a person died at least part of them went somewhere? Wasn't there a part of humans that was immortal and lived on at death? If that were true then what exactly happened to Lazarus when Jesus raised him from the dead? Did his soul or spirit come back somehow and reunite with his body?

These questions must have been a point of confusion for many more people as well because the next seminar topic would be a continuation of sorts from the previous meeting, but, with an interesting twist. After the preliminaries we opened our Bibles to Revelation chapter twelve, I had wondered when we would get back to the prophecies since this was supposed to be a Revelation Seminar. I would not have to wonder much longer. If you have not read it I would strongly recommend that you do. It is fascinating! In fact, Paul used it that very first night when he gave his overview of the Bible.

Revelation twelve is really the entire controversy between God and Satan in a nutshell. However, the chapter starts out describing a woman and a dragon. It is when you read this account that one should not take the passage literally, but prophetically. I knew this only because of the study with Paul.

Although there are many important elements to be examined, the evangelist immediately drew our attention to verses seven through nine. This is where John the Revelator wrote about the great battle in heaven. I know many of us have heard the story but it still deserves another look. As mentioned before, Karen and I had studied it with Paul but until then, I did not see the relationship the chapter had with the truth about death until that meeting.

The chapter tells of rebellion and subsequent war where Satan was cast out of heaven. We also learn in this passage that a third of the angels were deceived about the true nature of God and were cast out of heaven as well. Some wonder if this event actually happened. Some believe it did without question because of the spiritual battle that we see and feel all around us. Personally, I believe it by faith that the Bible is the true Word of God. Whatever your view, for developing a firm understanding of what happens to a person at death, I feel it is extremely important that we at least acknowledge a battle of some kind took place. And, that God's character was the main point of contention. One of the key points in this passage lies within verse nine of Revelation twelve which states…

> *And the great dragon was cast out, that old serpent, called the Devil, and Satan, which deceiveth the whole world: he was cast out into the earth, and his angels were cast out with him.* Rev. 12:9.

What we have here is who, why and even the what, as in what he does. But the how is the question. How would Satan deceive the whole world? Well, in many ways and all for the purpose of mischaracterizing the Creator. The approach of the evangelist on that cold February night in a small community center in Michigan would be to show what happened to the devil, and, what might be his motivation for continuing his deception. But where would he take us from here? He would take us back to Genesis. He would take us to the very beginning of the Bible on a search for Satan's first attempt in deceiving the whole world.

When we talk about the first lie we should make it clear that this would be the first lie used against humans on earth. Surely Satan lied in heaven as well when deceiving the angels. But in this context we want to discover how Satan deceives the whole world as the Bible says he does. Therefore, I use the term "the first lie" as being the first recorded earthly occurrence of blatant deception.

After God had created man and placed him in the garden, He explained that man may eat of any tree in the garden except for the tree of knowledge of good and evil. In a way you could look at the fact that God put this tree in the garden in the first place as a way of giving Adam the right to choose whether he wanted to follow God's way or not. This voting booth of sorts almost immediately disproved Satan's theory about God not giving all beings free will. Here is what we read about the devil's first lie in the book of Genesis, chapter three and verse one…

> *Now the serpent was more subtle than any beast of the field which the Lord God had made. And he said unto the woman, Yea, hath God said, Ye shall not eat of every tree of the garden? And the woman said unto the serpent, We may eat of the fruit of the trees of the garden: But the fruit of the tree which is in the*

midst of the garden, God hath said, Ye shall not eat of it, neither shall ye touch it, lest ye die. And the serpent said unto the woman, Ye shall not surely die: For God doth know that in the day ye eat thereof, then your eyes shall be opened, and ye shall be as gods, knowing good and evil. And when the woman saw that the tree was good for food, and that it was pleasant to the eyes, and a tree to be desired to make one wise, she took of the fruit thereof, and did eat, and gave also unto her husband with her; and he did eat. Genesis 3:1-6.

There it is. Not only was this the devil's first act of deception, but it was also the first time when he utilized another created being as a medium to do his dirty work. Adam was warned that he should not eat of that one tree because in that act of rebellion he would surely die. As we will touch on later, dying in this sense was not a physical death as we think of it today. Adam did not die right at the time of his disobedience. However, he would be separated from the Life Giver, and unless some provision would be made, Adam would remain eternally separated from God. This of course would ultimately lead to physical death with no chance of any form of eternal life. Basically, this idea that sin, or disobedience, is really like death because it separates us from the one who gives life, would be planted in my mind from then on.

As the evangelist expressed, the main point to grasp here was what God said, as opposed to what the devil had said. God told Adam that he would die because of his disobedience. And, of course, Satan told Eve that God was wrong and that they would not die, but become like gods. So who do we believe?

For my money God is the authority in this issue and He is the only One we should believe. He is the Creator and the Bible make's it clear that He alone can grant man immortality. ==Even though Adam and Eve may have been created with immortality, their disobedience separated them from God.== From that point on, all humans born in this world are not immortal, nor can we earn it.

This fact was confirmed by looking at what would be our last scripture of the night. We could see the above fact brought to view in this little understood passage. However, many have probably not studied this passage enough to see it. Unfortunately, even though many of us will openly deny that we believe Satan over God in this matter, we must admit that we all would like to believe that humans have eternal life already. But shouldn't we believe what the Bible really teaches?

Genesis chapter three, verses twenty-two and twenty-four states...

> *And the Lord God said, Behold, the man is become as one of us, to know good and evil: and now, <u>lest he put forth his hand, and take also of the tree of life, and eat, and live forever</u>: Therefore the Lord God sent him forth from the garden of Eden, to till the ground from whence he was taken. So he drove out the man; and he placed at the east of the garden of Eden Cherubims, and a flaming sword which turned everyway, to keep the way of the tree of life.*

Here is another foundation stone in our understanding of the truth about the dead. Eating from the knowledge of good and evil, will not make us gods and give us eternal life! Sure, one may have the knowledge and experience of obedience and disobedience, but this does not make us gods. Only when a person eats from the <u>Tree of Life</u> does one obtain eternal life.

So the sad story of Adam and Eve's rebellion ends in Genesis, chapter three, with God sending them out of the garden. Did He still love them? Sure He did. Would He make a way for them to have eternal life in the future? Yes He would. Will everyone have eternal life as a result of this plan? We would soon learn the answer.

As we attended the meetings this theme continued. What I learned was that the matters regarding life and death were so entwined in the words of the Bible I could hardly believe what I was learning. For the first time in my life I was finally feeling that the questions about faith started to make sense.

Everyone must believe in something. Even those who don't believe in a Grand Designer must have faith. Whether evolution or the big band theory, or whatever your cup of tea, faith just has to be a factor. Even those who believe that life ends at death must have faith in what they believe.

For my money, this world is just too beautiful, too perfect, too balanced to have just happened. I also believe that whoever created this perfection and all these creatures, created everything with a large dose of love and mercy- and maybe even a little dose of humor as well. If you agree with me about this world being created by a Loving Creator then I hope you will also agree that man was not an accident but a result of intelligent design. In fact, the Bible says we are made in God's image and in His likeness. But because of sin, man no longer has eternal life. We cannot earn it either. It is a free gift that can only be granted by God. I think most people will agree with the above statement. However, if you are reading this book from a non-Christian perspective, hopefully, you might find at least some logic in this view.

Logic has not always been a strong characteristic of mine. But when it came to finding a basis for learning about God, I needed logic to sort things out. Obviously, if the answers were only to be found in the spiritual realm, I wasn't going to find them. It is my belief that man cannot comprehend all the things of God except at a human level which he understands. If this were not so then those who aren't highly intellectual or spiritual wouldn't stand a chance, let alone those with mental disabilities. But contrary to popular belief, I feel God is there for everyone! And I also believe He is already working on our behalf. Maybe sometimes we stretch too far when He has been right there all the time.

I cannot claim that I really found anything, but that what I was seeking found me. Yes, God found me. He knew I needed to know the truth about this subject and I am convinced that in His wisdom, He orchestrated events and moved His spirit to use willing people in such a way as to create an opportunity for me to learn what I badly wanted to know. Did God shove me through the door? No, He didn't. Although reluctant at first, I walked through the door totally of my own free will.

Maybe you have needs and concerns that you have secretly murmured to God while already writing them off. Could it be possible that many of us make that mistake? Do we miss out on the things of God because we are reaching too far, thinking that He is in some far-away place? Or maybe we miss out because Satan works to counterfeit every honest presentation of truth or bogs us down with the cares of this world so much that we fail to see the answers to our problems. Could it be that the devil has so masterfully confused the world that we simply do not trust anyone, even the One who created us all? I'm sorry to say that this may be the case. But take it from me, God still does answer prayer. He will reveal Himself to those who humbly seek to know Him.

Being fully truthful I must say that I still had many questions after that couple of meetings about Lazarus and the first lie. But in addition to the meetings we were also fortunate to have received topic outlines with many scripture references for further study. These outlines, along with following through with the suggestion to purchase a concordance, helped us to feel relatively skilled to study virtually any topic on our own. And being able to study on our own was going to come in handy very soon.

Chapter 8

Aren't Human Soul's Immortal?

As much as we tried, we just could not make every meeting. We had missed a couple of nights following the one about the first lie but I do not remember the reasons why. Maybe the devil was working hard to keep us from going.

When we did attend again an elderly man asked a question at the start of the meeting. I was so glad the man asked this question because we had obviously missed one of the critical nights when this subject was being discussed. This person asked this question… "If man is not immortal, and he simply returns to the dust of the earth at death, what happens to the soul?" Great question! We would surely have to get the sermon notes on this one as I listened intently to the answer.

The response to this question was so simple that I couldn't believe it. The evangelist simply stated that the account of the creation of man is the exact opposite of what happens to a person at death. Then, he asked us to open our Bibles to the book of Genesis once again. This time we would read from chapter two and verse seven.

And God formed man out of the dust of the earth and breathed into his nostrils the breath of life, and man became the living soul.

Then the evangelist took us to the book of Ecclesiastes. I had never heard of that one before but would surely return to it again, especially chapter twelve, and verse seven.

Then shall the dust return to the earth as it was: and the spirit shall return unto God who gave it.

On the surface these two examples didn't do it for me, that is, until the evangelist told us that the breath of life in Genesis had the same meaning as the word spirit used in this passage of Ecclesiastes. Then it was explained this way. Just like a light bulb plus electricity equals a lighted bulb, so it is with the creation of man. As God formed man from the dust of the earth, and breathed into man the breath of life, man *became a living soul.* In other words, the breath from God gives life to this body made from the elements with all of its thoughts and functions. Therefore, a soul is brought into existence at the point when it is given the breath of life. On the reverse, when it comes to death, the exact opposite happens. The body, or dust, goes back into the earth while the breath, or spirit, goes back to God.

Obviously, I would have to do more study on this subject but what I heard made sense. Basically, what the evangelist was saying was that there was no such thing as a dead soul. I had heard people say, ashes to ashes and dust to dust at funerals; maybe this is what they meant. One thing was for sure, the idea that man does not have some third element fit perfectly with the story of Lazarus.

The evangelist had given a satisfactory answer to the man's question. Well, at least it seemed that way to me. But as we had been advised to do so many times during these meetings, I would study this topic for myself in greater depth. Not only did I want to make sure we had not been lead astray, but I just had to dig deeper. Even though I didn't really have a big problem with what was being said, this stuff was just so much different than anything I had ever heard. Therefore, I just had to check it out because I simply could not be truly satisfied until I could get total peace of mind on the subject.

During the rest of the meeting all I could think about was what I might have missed. Of all the nights I should have attended, the previous meeting was it. How could I make up for that lost time? Fortunately, there were those sermon notes and we also learned there would be audio tapes available later as well.

At the end of this meeting which was on the law of God, Karen remembered to grab the sermon notes for the nights we missed. I could hardly wait to find out more about the breath and spirit being one in the same along with any other jewels that I could. Like I stated earlier, the purchase of a concordance helped us become somewhat skilled in looking up many words and where those words could be found in the Bible. So, the next night after work I started taking the foundation that was given to us thus far to the next level.

With the information we received the previous night, learning more about the references to the body and the spirit was sort of fun. Sure, I had heard about the basic Christian concept of man being formed from the dust, but the rest of it, well, I really didn't have a clue. But like the Bereans in the Bible who studied after being taught by the Apostle Paul, we too needed to check things out for ourselves. And of course, I would encourage anyone reading this book to do the same. In fact, this book is a testimony meant to show that you don't have to be a theologian or scholar to understand Bible truths.

Questioning Death

It simply takes a little guidance to get started, an honest heart, and a big dose of the Holy Spirit.

Using the concordance I was able to do a thorough study from just about every angle and every word I could think of relating to death. I looked up the words dust, breath, spirit, sleep, grave, and even soul in an attempt to get a well rounded understanding. And I'll admit, none of this would have been possible without the guidance of Paul and the meetings.

When you read these clear passages, keep in mind this is only a small snapshot of the many references for each word. But as you will see, they clearly supported what we had learned so far.

2 Samuel 7:12 And when thy days be fulfilled, and thou shall sleep with thy fathers, I will set up thy seed after thee...

Job 7:9,10 As the cloud is consumed and vanisheth away: so he that goeth down to the grave shall come up no more. He shall return no more to his house, neither shall his place know him any more.

Job 7:21 And why dost thou not pardon my transgression, and take away mine iniquity? For now shall I sleep in the dust; and thou shalt seek me in the morning, but I shall not be.

Job 21:26 They shall lie down alike in the dust, and the worms shall cover them... verse 32... Yet shall he be brought to the grave, and shall remain in the tomb.

Psalm 13:3 Consider and hear me, O Lord my God: lighten mine eyes, lest I sleep the sleep of death;

Psalm 115:17 *The dead praise not the Lord, neither any that go down into silence.*

Psalm 146:4 *His breath goeth forth, he returneth to his earth; in that very day his thoughts perish.*

Ecclesiastes 9:10 *Whatsoever thy hand findeth to do, do it with all thy might; for there is no work, nor device, nor knowledge, nor wisdom, in the grave, whither thou goest.*

And then of course I'll throw in these two that the evangelist mentioned...

Genesis 2:7 *And the Lord God formed man of the dust of the ground, and breathed into his nostrils the breath of life; and man became a living soul.*

Ecclesiastes 12:7 *Then shall the dust return to the earth as it was: and the spirit shall return unto God who gave it.*

When you look up the many references to the word soul in the concordance you find quite a few. However, most references to the "soul" are all about the living and not the dead. A good example of the living being referred to as a "souls" is in the book of Acts where the Bible tells us that after listening to the teachings of Peter about Jesus, many accepted what they had heard.

Acts 2:41 *Then they that gladly received his word were baptized: and the same day there were added unto them about three thousand souls.*

Then in verse 43…

And fear came upon every soul: and many wonders and signs were done by the apostles.

What I learned by using the concordance was quite interesting. Not only did the Bible confirm that people are souls but I also learned that the word soul is also used to mean the animated part of man. In fact, the word can be use to describe other living creatures as well. But the word is never used to describe man being immortal. The Bible speaks of living people as souls. And when you think about it, most of us have heard statements like… "oh, that poor soul" or, "she's a happy soul." Therefore, this means that ==the soul and the spirit are not the same.== You see, the Bible says that the breath, or spirit of God goes back to God at death. And, once the breath is gone, the soul will cease to have life.

But just to be totally objective on this issue, take a look at this one that gave me some trouble.

Revelation 20:4-6 And I saw thrones, and they that sat upon them, and judgment was given unto them: and I saw the <u>souls of them that were beheaded for the witness of Jesus</u>, and for the word of God, and which had not worshiped the beast, neither his image, neither had received his mark upon their foreheads, or in their hands; and <u>they lived and reigned with Christ a thousand years</u>. But the rest of the dead lived not again until the thousand years were finished. <u>This is the first resurrection.</u> Blessed and holy is he that hath part in the first resurrection: on such the second death hath no power, but they shall be priests of God and of Christ, and shall reign with him a thousand years.

This one can be a little hard to understand so I have underlined what I felt were significant parts of this passage. On first glance it seems to say that John saw the souls of the dead. But a closer look tells us that these beheaded martyrs for Jesus will be raised in the first resurrection. Then, after the thousand years have passed, the rest of the dead, or wicked, will be resurrected. Another important part of this passage is the fact that these souls did not worship the beast or receive a mark on their foreheads or hands. If souls are like a ghost or spirit, would they have foreheads to receive a mark? Not likely. What John saw here was simply people who were martyred and resurrected in the first resurrection.

There is one more passage that I ran across when looking for the references to the word soul. This one also caused me to wonder about the possibility of souls being immortal. And it's a good thing I had a concordance for this one. It is found in the book of Matthew, chapter ten, and verse twenty-eight. Jesus said...

"And fear not them which kill the body, but are not able to kill the soul: but rather fear him which is able to destroy both soul and body in hell."

Even though Jesus clearly states here that the soul can be destroyed in hell, I was confused about what he meant by being able to kill the body but not the soul. Was he saying that the soul could still exist apart from the body? Again, I was happy to have a concordance to refer to because I was able to compare the word soul as used in this passage to how it was used in others. The interesting thing about the word soul as used here is that it comes from the Hebrew word "psuche" which is translated to mean life in other passages. In fact, in over forty other passages the same word is translated into the word life. Here's just one...

> Matthew 16:25 *Whosoever shall lose his life [psuche] for my sake shall find it.*

If the word soul was used in the place of the word life in the above passage, the text would not make sense. This is because the text would be saying that people could lose their soul for Christ's sake. However, the use of the word life in place of the word soul in Matthew 10:28 makes perfect sense and is consistent with the rest of the Bible. The real issue here is who can kill the physical life, and who has the power to grant eternal life. And, just to better understand this passage, it was easy enough to simply compare it to one of the other gospels.

> Luke: 12:4,5 *And I say unto you my friends, Be not afraid of them that kill the body, and after that have no more that they can do. But I will forewarn you whom you shall fear: Fear him, which after he hath killed hath power to cast into hell.*

In Luke's account of the words of Jesus, he uses the lesson but does not use the words "kills the soul." Instead he says "cast in hell." This is because they mean the same thing. Men can only kill the body and take away the physical life. God, on the other hand, is the only one who can give us eternal life. In this case, not only would a wicked person's body be destroyed in hellfire, but their lives would be snuffed out for all eternity.

This little bit of detective work was typical of how the Bible will interpret itself given the right guidance and an open heart. By this time my attitude was truly turning around. I really was starting to feel it was possible for someone like me to know the Bible better and maybe even know the whole truth about what happens to those who have died.

Chapter 9

What About the Spirit?

While examining the word *spirit* in an attempt to find its true meaning, what we found was the word is used in basically five ways. Why is this? There is a strong possibility that the English language simply did not include words that would cover each and every meaning necessary. Therefore the interpreters most likely used the word *spirit* in a broad and generic way. Do any of the uses of this word point to the conclusion that humans have immortal spirits? Let's find out.

The five basic uses of the word spirit are these...

> The breath of life
> A person's disposition or thoughts
> Evil spirits
> The Holy Spirit
> The person themselves

First we will look at the spirit being the breath of God, or in other words, what gives a person life. And again I ask you to keep in mind that anyone can do this. These are basically the passages I found using a concordance and a little common sense.

Job 27:3 *All the while my breath is in me the spirit of God is in my nostrils.*

Eccl 8:8 *There is no man that hath power over the spirit to retain the spirit; neither hath he power in the day of death:*

Eccl 12:7 *Then shall the dust return to the earth as it was: and the spirit shall return unto God who gave it.*

Ezek 37:14 *And I shall put my spirit in you, and ye shall live...*

James 2:26 *For as the body without the spirit is dead, so faith without works is dead also.*

Here are examples of the word used to describe a person's disposition or thoughts.

Prov 16:19 *Better it is to be of a humble spirit with the lowly...*

Prov 17:22 *A merry heart doeth good like a medicine: but a broken spirit drieth the bones.*

Eccl 7:8 *Better is the end of a thing than the beginning thereof: and the patient in spirit is better than the proud in spirit.*

Isa 66:2 *...but to this man I will look, even to him that is poor and of a contrite spirit.*

1 Cor 5:3 *For I verily, as absent in body, but present in spirit, have judged already, as though I were present...*

Eph 4:23 *And be renewed in the spirit of your mind...*

And here we have a few examples of the word spirit used in relation to evil spirits.

Acts 19:15,16 *And the evil spirit answered and said, Jesus I know, and Paul I know; but who are ye? And the man in whom the evil spirit was leaped on them...*

Luke 7:21 *And in that same hour he cured many of their infirmities and plagues, and of evil spirits: and unto many that were blind he gave sight.*

Luke 8:29,30 *For he had commanded the unclean spirit to come out of the man, For oftentimes it had caught him: and he was kept bound with chains and fetters; and he brake the bands, and was driven of the devil into the wilderness. And Jesus asked him, saying, What is thy name? And he said, Legion: because many devils were entered into him.*

Rev 18:2 *...Babylon the great is fallen, is fallen, and is become the habitation of devils, and the hold of every foul spirit...*

Here is the word spirit used in reference to the Holy Spirit. (often in capital letters)

Ps 51:11 *Cast me not away from thy presence; and take not thy holy spirit from me.*

Isa 48:16 *...the Lord God, and his Spirit hath sent me.*

Ezek 11:5 *And the Spirit of the Lord fell upon me, and said unto me, Speak...*

Matt 3:16 *And Jesus, when he was baptized, went up straightway out of the water: and, lo, the heavens were opened unto him, and he saw the Spirit of God descending like a dove, and lighting upon him...*

Luke 4:18 *The Spirit of the Lord is upon me, because he hath anointed me to preach the gospel to the poor...*

Luke 11:13 *If ye then, being evil, know how to give good gifts unto your children: how much more shall your heavenly Father give the Holy Spirit to them that ask him?*

John 16:13 *Howbeit when he, the Spirit of truth, is come, he will guide you into all truth...*

Rom 8:14 *For as many as are lead by the Spirit of God, they are the sons of God.*

The examples of the word spirit used to mean a person are few but can be found.

Ezek 21:7 *...and every heart shall melt, and all hand shall be feeble, and every spirit shall faint, and all knees shall be weak as water...*

2 Pet 3:18-20 *For Christ also hath once suffered for sins, the just for the unjust, that he might bring us to God, being put to death in the flesh, but quickened by*

the Spirit: By which also he went and preached unto the spirits in prison: Which sometimes were disobedient, when once the longsuffering of God waited in the days of Noah, while the ark was a preparing, wherein few, that is, eight souls were saved by water.

This last passage is often used in an attempt to show that Jesus went to hell to preach to the spirits of the dead after His death on the cross. However, a clear reading shows that this is not at all the case. What the passage actually says is that Jesus was quickened, or made alive, by the spirit of God. And, through this same spirit, or Holy spirit, He pleaded with people who were in the bondage of sin and rebellion at the time prior to the flood.

There are many other passages in which various uses of the word spirit can be shown. This small list was given to show that the word spirit does not mean some separate and immortal entity of man. Are some passages a little confusing? Sure they are. But when you get the complete picture and use a majority of texts on a given topic or word to lead you to the true meaning, you will be rewarded.

Does this mean that I don't believe in evil spirits or demon spirits? No, I do. In fact, the Bible tells us that the spirits of devils, or fallen angels, are Satan's workers that specifically work to deceive people on earth. How do they do that? Basically, by impersonating people, or by using people directly. I know this might sound a little strange or scary, but we will share what the Bible says about this in a later chapter. So stay tuned!

As Karen and I continued to study in an attempt to tackle this issue of death from every angle, we attended more meetings. And of course, we still had more questions. Space does not allow me to cover all of our movements, thoughts and emotions during the next few weeks and months. If I could describe my mood in a couple of words, I would have to say

I was cautiously excited. More and more I was becoming convinced that people simply did not receive their reward upon death. But the rest of the world believed otherwise. Was it stressful? Yes. Especially in light of what I just mentioned about evil spirits who try to use others to distract, deceive and discourage. I believe this happens when they know you are getting close to being dangerous because of what God was doing in your life. Yes, there was quite the spiritual battle going on that I did not fully recognize until well after going through it.

Was I at least a little scared? No, not exactly. There were times when I was very scared. This stuff is real. Was it all worth it? Absolutely! The more the issue became clear, the more I knew which side I wanted to be on. But the devil wasn't going to let us go easily.

Chapter 10

When Does A Person Go To Heaven?

    I hope you can see how this issue becomes easier to understand when you start to look at all of the evidence. We had learned that the words of Jesus in the story of Lazarus along with the many other passages prove that death is like a sleep until the resurrection. In addition, we learned that at death, the dust returns to the earth and the breath returns to God who gave it. And, when we read that in the grave, men cannot praise God or work, and that their thoughts perish, much of the mystery about death was being removed.

    Even though we were beginning to get a pretty good handle on the Bible teaching about death, I still had lots of questions. The information was definitely a blessing to me and many others who had learned this for the first time. However, I still had many things that needed clarification. I guess love and concern for my brother and not knowing his true standing with God at the time of his death made me feel that I had to get this right. Honestly, the thought of the dead being in the dust of the earth and all that wasn't very comforting either. And how about all those people that I had assumed were already in heaven?

Believe me, I was sympathetic to the idea that most people would much rather believe that their loved ones were in heaven. I must say, my brother being in heaven is much more pleasant to think about as opposed to the possible alternatives. Maybe that's why preachers usher everyone into heaven at funerals. But was that really the truth? And was the fate of good people the same as those that were, well, not so good? Do we all just go to the grave and await a resurrection like in the story of Lazarus? Are the wicked in the grave as well? Or, are they being tortured in the center of the earth? The answers to those questions are not only clearly presented in the words of Jesus and the Bible writers but the issue even becomes more clear when we can lay aside our many years of preconceived ideas. This may be a chore for some but it wasn't really a problem for me.

I was not fully convinced of anything in particular about death when this journey began, other than the fact that I thought death was a bad thing. Therefore, I basically had nothing major to consider other than what I had heard from others. Even though I thought I was becoming fairly knowledgeable by now, anything was still possible as far as I was concerned. Heaven, hell, purgatory, reincarnation, back to dust, ghosts, spirits, all these words and thoughts were still floating around in my mind. I knew something had to happen, but I just didn't have all the pieces sorted out quite yet. Quite frankly, there were so many weird and potentially unexplainable elements of this issue to consider that I still was somewhat skeptical that anyone, especially someone like me, could ever be certain. But I was determined to keep going.

From the very start of all this we had been told that to truly understand any Bible subject, the best way was to look at all of the relevant text and simply allow the Bible to interpret itself. Then, if there are any texts which appear to contradict the rest, those text can then be understood in the context of the others. So we tried it.

Did the idea that the dead being in a state of sleep fit with other Bible passages? If so, did that mean that humans do not immediately experience their ultimate destiny upon death? The many text relating to the dust and spirit seemed convincing enough, but was there more? It did not take long to find some pretty strong proof that what we were learning was true. Just take a look at these tremendous words from the Apostle Paul about those that are asleep. ...

> 1 Corinthians 15:51-57 *Behold, I shew you a mystery; we shall not all sleep, but we shall all be changed, In a moment, in the twinkling of an eye, at the last trump: for the trumpet shall sound, and the dead shall be raised incorruptible, and we shall be changed. For this corruptible must put on incorruption, and this mortal must put on immortality. So when this corruptible shall have put on incorruption, and this mortal shall have put on immortality, then shall be brought to pass the saying that is written, Death is swallowed up in victory. O death, where is thy sting? O grave, where is thy victory? The sting of death is sin; and the strength of sin is the law. But thanks be to God, which giveth us the victory through our Lord Jesus Christ.*

Wow! These corruptible and mortal bodies of ours will <u>become</u> incorruptible and immortal. What a statement. And when will this happen? At the last trump. Notice also the reference to God as it says that through Jesus we gain the victory over death. That's good news! And it also said that we shall not all sleep, but we will all be changed. I believe this to be a reference to the fact that there will be some that will be alive at "the last trump." But can this be confirmed?

This next passage may be the clincher for many. It surely was for me.

> 1 Thessalonians 4:13-18 *But I would not have you to be ignorant, brethren, concerning them which are asleep, that ye sorrow not, even as others which have no hope. For if we believe that Jesus died and rose again, even so them also which sleep in Jesus will God bring with him. For this we say unto you by the word of the Lord, that we which are alive and remain unto the coming of the Lord shall not prevent them which are asleep. For the Lord himself shall descend from heaven with a shout, with the voice of the archangel, and with the trump of God: <u>and the dead in Christ shall rise first</u>: Then we which are alive and remain shall be caught up together with them in the clouds, to meet the Lord in the air: and so shall we ever be with the Lord. Wherefore, comfort one another with these words.*

When I first read this passage I felt that Paul was speaking directly to me. Not only would I have considered myself ignorant about those which were asleep, but there was a time when I really didn't have much hope and I needed to be comforted as well. I needed to know what happens at death. Not only that, but I wanted to know what happens beyond death, if anything.

This last text clearly showed that if we believe Jesus died and rose from the dead, then those who were asleep in him would be raised and brought to heaven with him. When? At the last trump, at the time of his coming.

These truths began to have a profound impact on me. Other than the obvious points like "the dead in Christ shall rise first," I began to see the correlation between the last trump, the trump of God, the second coming of Jesus with a shout and how it all tied together with the story of Lazarus. Do you remember what Martha said to Jesus in John 11:24? She knew Lazarus would live again *"in the resurrection at the last day."* This is even more evidence for believing that people do not receive their reward, or punishment, immediately upon death.

We will use the method of comparing scripture to scripture and look at the last day in a little more depth in just a moment but I just have to make this point. I believe that we learned something else very significant in First Thessalonians chapter four that should not be missed. For many today who believe the rapture of the church will be some secret event, you may want to take another look at what the Bible really teaches. I mention this because a shout, the voice of the archangel and the trump of God do not sound to me like things that happen in secret. Do they? We will come back to this issue later in this book but I just wanted to plant a seed here for your consideration.

Now back to those that are asleep being raised at the last day. When I looked to the concordance for those words and where they are used I found again that they support what Paul said. Here are just a few statements from the mouth of Jesus himself as written in John, chapter six.

John 6:40 *And this is the will of him that sent me, that every one that seeth the Son, and believeth on him, may have everlasting life: and I will raise him up at the last day.*

John 6:44 *No man can come to me, except the Father which hath sent me draw him: and I will raise him up at the last day.*

John 6:54 *Whoso eateth my flesh, and drinketh my blood, (reference to accepting Jesus and to the Lord's* supper), *hath eternal life; and I will raise him up at the last day.*

And here's another that again strongly points to when people will be raised.

1 Corinthians 15:21-23 For since by man came death, by man also came the resurrection of the dead. For as in Adam all die, even so in Christ shall all be made alive. But every man in his own order: Christ the first fruits; afterward they that are Christ's at his coming.

And just take a look at this one from the book of John…

John 5:28,29 Marvel not at this: for the hour is coming, in the which all that are in the graves shall hear his voice, And shall come forth; they that have done good, unto the resurrection of life; and they that have done evil, unto the resurrection of damnation.

Are there more scriptures that point to the same conclusion? Sure there are. But I think you can see why I don't have to spend a lot of time giving all of the supporting scriptures I came upon. This is mainly because I simply could not find any contradictions. However, I have said this before and I will continue to say this… I encourage each reader to get into the Bible for themselves. What you will find is that the more you prayerfully study, the more you will see the beauty of the Bible. The beauty you will find is not only in the logic and consistency, but in the message. Quite simply, God loves all mankind and he has planned a heavenly reward for each and every person. But as we would soon learn, not every person will choose to accept the gift God offers. Why? I believe it is because they really don't know Him.

Chapter 11

Does It Really Matter What I Believe?

Before I learned this stuff, if someone had told me that my loved ones were not in heaven, I would have been very upset! Not only that, but I probably would have denied the suggestion. In addition, I most likely would have determined that the person presenting these lies was being very mean and insensitive, judgmental, and probably off their rocker. So, if you haven't thrown this book away by now, I am very proud of you. It is a very hard thing to question your entire spiritual foundation even if that foundation was a little shaky. And I believe with all my heart that by hanging in there, you will be greatly rewarded.

It should not be a big surprise to us that most of the world has been deceived by the devil. This is not something that I came up with but I sure believe it to be true. I believe it because that's what the Bible tells us. Revelation 12:9. In fact, the text actually states that devil deceives the whole world. Because of this, I understand that many will probably reject the idea that death is a sleep until Jesus returns.

If God's word tells us that the body returns to the earth and spirit goes back to God, then what exactly is the part of us that would go to heaven like so many believe? And, if there is part of a person that goes to heaven, then what exactly would that part do? Without a body or the breath of life, and without any thoughts, what could we do? Would we have any senses like sight or hearing and be able to see the beauty of heaven? How about earth, would it really be heaven if we could see the pain and suffering of loved ones we left behind?

We can even take this a little further by asking this question: Would it really be heaven if we had knowledge of people burning in hell? If we are honest with ourselves we simply have to consider these things if we believe in the immortality of the soul. If we believe that ghosts are actually the souls of the dead, doesn't that mean they can see everything that happens? I apologize for asking so many questions but you have to admit that you have probably asked some of these same questions yourself.

But let's think about this issue of what would be burning if there were wicked people burning in hell right now. If their bodies are in the grave then does that mean their souls are burning? What good would it do to burn something that can not feel it? I looked into this question just to see if it fit with death being a sleep. Here is what I found in the book of Job.

> Job 21:28-32 *For ye say, where is the house of the prince? And where are the dwelling places of the wicked? Have ye not asked them that go by the way? And do ye not know their tokens? That the wicked is reserved to the day of destruction? they shall be brought forth to the day of wrath? Who shall declare his way to his face? And who shall repay him what he*

hath done? Yet shall he be brought to the grave, and shall remain in the tomb.

That was just about all I needed on that one. The wicked will be brought to the grave and remain in the tomb, reserved to the day of destruction. It all seemed pretty straight forward to me.

Even though I was once very confused about God, I now believe in a loving Creator who gave us the Bible so that we could know Him better. And because of this, I should study His word and believe what it says. There is really no way around it. On the other hand, if the devil is truly the enemy of God, and he knows the Bible is the true Word of God, then the devil would do anything to counterfeit its teachings, or even distract people from reading it. And, if Satan is the father of lies, just think of the implications if he tries to convince the world that people go directly to heaven, or hell, if they really don't. What a mess.

Let's think for a moment about a young mother, a good person who died in a tragic accident leaving a teenager girl behind. Consider what might go through the mind of this young woman who misses mom so much. Would she be angry with God? Will anyone be able to help her when she is considering suicide? ==What a shame that this beautiful young woman believes that taking her own life is the only way because the pain will stop and she will be where mommy is. Or will she? Can you see how the devil works?==

I often wonder how long my sweet Aunt Eva would have lived, and if I could have gotten to know her better before she died. But I didn't have much of a chance. You see, my Aunt Eva was found in her car with the garage door closed within a few months after her husband and life-long friend, Uncle Mickey died. What a tragedy. But you know, I didn't think that way at the time but simply reasoned that she probably missed him too much to go on and probably believed she would be seeing her loved one immediately.

Who really knows what goes on in the minds of those who have lost loved ones. Everyone is different. I know it sure messed me up for a while. But I wonder, would Aunt Eva have committed suicide if she knew that Uncle Mickey was not yet in heaven but was actually asleep in the grave until Jesus comes?

As I was learning more about this subject and the many implications of following the devil's lie, the possibilities were overwhelming. It seemed to me that the pain cause by simply not knowing what happens actually makes a loved one's death much harder to deal with. And, the more I contemplated the matter, the more I realized what a masterful job the devil had done.

Clearly, the deception about the state of the dead is part of the devil's continuing plan to misrepresent the true character of God. And when you think about it, it's a perfect plan. Here's how. As the devil has contaminated the world with sin and rebellion he has also orchestrated things in such a way that if someone dies, God gets the blame. In addition, as the devil gets people to believe that when you die you go straight to heaven because all humans are endowed with some sort of immortal component, then why would anyone need to honor God and the salvation He offers?

If you have followed any of the recent news reports then you most likely have seen the many tragedies known as suicide bombings. Is it possible that a misunderstanding of God's character and a belief that people go immediately to heaven at death could be the basis for these bombings? Dear friend, it is not only possible, but probable.

I believe that devil-deceived men teach lies about the nature of man and brainwash weak and vulnerable young people. Yes, these misguided recruiters convince their sacrificial volunteers to commit these crimes in the name of god as they offer irresistible promises. What young person would turn down money and life in paradise for their families, a Martyrs reward in heaven including seventy virgins, and a chance to meet the prophets and their friends in heaven?

I don't know if I am sorry, or not sorry to tell them that it's all a big lie. They will not go to heaven. Nor will they receive any of the other rewards. And the really sad thing about all this is these men believe that killing people is actually God's will! In addition, they also believe they are doing their so-called infidels victims a favor. Oh friend, if only the Christian church would see what is happening and study their Bibles! Maybe then they could truly change the world by telling people the truth. God does not want any human being to kill another. Nor do people receive any of the rewards promised, especially rewards like seventy virgins. But Satan is a smart one. Yes, he knows how to tempt young men and boys. To be real honest, this stuff turns my stomach and I am angry with what the devil is doing.

No wonder why many in the world today cry out to God when they see what is happening. The sad thing is, many curse God because they think He could somehow be involved in this culture of death. And as stated before, even within the ranks of the Christian churches today many believe the same sort of lies. Yes, many young people have committed suicide to be with loved ones, or because they simply do not see the purpose of life on earth. They may have been told about God, but they have a tough time justifying a relationship with someone who might burn them forever because they feel like they are not worthy.

After considering all of this kind of information I had to ask myself these obvious questions. Who do I think has planted the seeds of doubt in the minds of people on earth about the true character of God? Who is it that wants us to deny that God so loved the world that He gave His only Begotten Son? Who is it that wants us to be confused about what the Bible teaches? Who is it that wants the world to think that the Bible is not true when it clearly states that God is not willing that any would perish?

I hope you understand why I no longer wonder about all of this confusion. The devil is very serious about his work. There is really no other explanation for it. As I studied this subject more and more I learned that there are two sides and two sides only. On one side we have the truth of God's word. Then we have all that other stuff; an eternally burning hell, ghosts or the souls of the dead roaming the earth, prayers to and for the souls of the dead, reincarnation and the list of implications goes on and on.

Some believe that they are on a path of former and after lives that will ultimately lead to perfection. Some believe that at death they must first go through a place of limbo, or purgatory, where they will be purified before being deemed worthy for heaven. But when you break it all down, many of these supposed paths to paradise, or nirvana, or wherever, make the Creator's plan virtually insignificant.

It truly matters what we believe about death, heaven, hell and God. This is not just some game, even though it may be for Satan. I would have to say that it mattered to my Grandfather, my Brother, my aunt Eva, and many others. It matters to mothers young and old, suicide bombers, those on death row, and to those in nursing homes. It matters to people everywhere in this world and to the angels in heaven. And most of all, it matters to Our Heavenly Father and the Son that He sent to die for our death. Without this sacrifice none of us would ever have that chance to "put on immortality."

Chapter 12

What About Near Death Experiences?

*A*t the time when we studied this issue relating to the state of the dead, near death experiences were one of those questions that seemed to contradict the Bible teachings. To be honest I could not find anything in the Bible that discusses the issue. This alone told me a lot.

Near death experiences are probably quite fascinating to those who have gone through such a thing. But the question is… what are they actually experiencing? Does clinical death really mean they are dead? Did their soul or spirit truly depart from their bodies and hover over the doctors frantically attempting to revive them? Was God playing some kind of joke on them to scare, or tease them? What were they actually experiencing when they described seeing a bright light and having a feeling of indescribable peace? Was it really heaven? Or, was their subconscious simply allowing them to see what they believed they were expecting to see? Could it even be that the devil is helping them along a little in their thinking?

I wonder sometimes if the people who claim to have had such experiences also claim a close relationship with God. Or, if they even think having a relationship with Jesus is important. Maybe these people already believed that all people go to heaven and they mistake the bright light of the operating room table to what they believe heaven will be like. Personally I have seen a few movies myself that paint heaven as a place with a bright light and clouds and fog and people dressed in pure white. Who knows, maybe people who think they will die prepare themselves for what might happen based on some movie they saw. Sure, its nice to believe that we are all good and no matter what we do we will get a nice reward at death. But is it true?

Personally, I believe that these people really didn't die. How can I say that? Because, they were alive to tell about it, and because the Bible makes what happens pretty clear. At death, the breath of life goes back to God. Not partway back, all the way back. I am not an expert in this area so I cannot really know what happens to those to claim to have seen the other side. But what I do know is that this is just another one of those issues that confuses people. Especially in light of the fact that these people really didn't die. I also find it strange that the Bible doesn't have much, if anything, to say about the subject.

One of the main reasons I got onboard this train in the first place was because of confusing issues like near death experiences. Deep down inside I just knew that God didn't want me to be confused. Thanks to Him what I have come to know has brought me comfort.

And you know what the really great thing about this is? It is so simple when you get right down to it. For me, and I hope for you, following this new line of thinking is just so logical! How simple and logical? Let me walk you through it.

I believe that humans did not evolve but were created by an Intelligent Designer. And, if this is true, then whoever created us must have loved us an awful lot to have also created all of the beauty in the world we see. It also makes sense to accept the idea that this Creator would love His creatures as if they were His children. Now if this Creator was like a loving Father and His children went astray, logic tells me that He would allow them to make that choice. But I believe He would also make a way for them to return if they found themselves off the good path and desired to get back to the right one again. This Father might even make sacrifices for these children and maybe even make the ultimate sacrifice so that they could be reconciled with Him once again. And if it were true that He would make such a sacrifice, wouldn't it stand to reason that He would want us to know the truth about death? I think so. You see, creation, children going astray, sacrifice, and love are basically the theme of the Bible. Its not even basically the theme of the Bible, it *is* the theme of the Bible! And it sure doesn't sound very confusing to me.

So how did things get so messed up? Quite simply, discontent and rebellion started the whole thing. Most people would agree that if you believe in God and you have faith in His word then you must accept what it says about rebellion and its consequences. Otherwise, how could we possibly explain this state that the world is in today? This writer is not highly educated, nor any type of biblical scholar. I am just a simple man who understands that God, and others, are responsible for my success and what knowledge I have. It's hard to say how many people will ultimately read this book. Maybe because I lack a fancy title or a long list of impressive credentials nobody will. Who knows? All I can hope is that if anyone does, maybe in some small way the reader might become at least a little more enlightened and encouraged to study on their own. Of course, my real hope is that that they will be greatly enlightened, liberated by the truth, and be in heaven someday!

Everyone should ask themselves if they are really comfortable with their belief system. I know I wasn't. It's not that my parents and grandparents were bad people or anything. In fact, they probably did the best they could with what they knew. The funny thing is, I thought I was fine too, for awhile. Maybe it's the same for most people. But when a tragedy enters your life, that's when you realize things aren't so right after all.

Bad things are happening to people every day. And sometimes you just can't help but to be disgusted with it all. I believe we are all born with a desire to want peace and a connection with God. We want to know we are here for a reason, and that we are important. And if we do not know where else to go to get that connection we find other ways to cope, or imagine that we are somehow connected. For some it's drugs, for others alcohol. For many we seek solace in some form of spiritual enlightenment. But here is the rub: Who do we get our information from? Do we get it from ourselves, television, taro cards, horoscopes, Ouji boards or talking to the dead? How about getting the answers from those who claim to have seen the other side? I believe all of these choices will lead us into many wrong directions simply because they are all so inconsistent in their message. And when you begin to understand the basics that we have discussed in this book you should be able to see that these are all just counterfeits to God's word.

If all the above are just counterfeits, why doesn't God just reveal the truth to everybody? He is God, so why can't He do that? As I stated early in this book, I wondered the same thing. But I have learned three very important lessons. First, God does not force the accepting of Himself upon anyone. Secondly, Satan has played upon man's free will by creating so many deceptions that many people simply don't have a clue where to start. And third, the longer a person lives, the more prideful and protective they become. Therefore,

Questioning Death

a drastic deprogramming has to occur before they can see through the lies, smoke and mirrors.

Even though God does not force His will upon anyone it may be unfair to assume that He has taken a passive roll in all of this. Quite the contrary, God has revealed to us the entire scope of this issue through His word. Inspired by the Holy Spirit, His chosen scribes have penned every detail of what we need to know. But the problem is that not very many take the time to study what the Bible really has to reveal to them. I know this to be true because I was in that boat. Yes, most people assume they know what they need to know as passed down from generation to generation, or as learned through listening to some professional preacher.

One of the most amazing things about all of this to me is that while people are fooled into thinking they have a handle on life, and death, they continue to be fascinated by those who have claimed to have knowledge of the other side. But who, if any of those who have claimed such an experience, describe heaven in the way the Bible describes heaven? Not even one of them. That's right there is never any mention of God, the angels, the tree of life or streets of gold. No mansions, saints, thrones or singing, nothing. It's as if they never really got there, as if there was some mistake. But from what I have learned, God is not in the business of playing games with people's lives like some twisted puppet master.

If anyone would have been able to give an accurate report from the other side, wouldn't it have been Lazarus? But we find no such report from Lazarus, Jesus, nor from anyone else for that matter. Why is this? Because people cannot die and come back to report that there is an immediate reward after death!

Just in case you might have been thinking that near death experiences throw a monkey wrench into all that has been written in this book, think again. I'll admit this was a tough one to reason through and I did not have the answer at this time. But in the same way that I was lead to a logical understanding about the rest, I hoped the Bible would come through for us again. So I continued to study this subject while observing the world, something that I still do today. I've seen many programs and read many newspapers, books and magazine articles about lost souls, ghosts, near death experiences, and mediums communicating with the dead and everything in between. In fact, I had even tried to communicate with my brother. The difference with my method and the rest was that I did not use any fancy hocus pocus. I simply tried to talk with him, audibly. But you know what? He didn't talk back.

Was it possible that he could hear me but he simply didn't bother to talk back? Maybe he didn't respond because I wasn't the best of brothers and God wouldn't let him. Or, maybe he really could hear me and tried to make contact, but for some reason, he couldn't. I believe that many people wonder about such things as I did. And I also believe that even today, because of our desperation to know if our loved ones are safe, we will seek answers through almost every possible source. Oh yes, many people either believe in, or engage in practices designed to contact the dead. But in doing so, are they inviting deception and flirting with disaster?

As we enter some very critical chapters of this book and tackle even harder issues, I must ask that you remember two things. First, God loves you and He wants you to know the truth. And secondly, Satan does not want you to love God, nor does he want you to know the truth about those who have died.

Chapter 13

Can Visitations Be Explained?

The meetings at the little community center had passed but we continued to study with Paul as well as on our own. Both Karen and I felt we had learned many things but knew there was still so much that we didn't know. However, at least now we were feeling equipped to take a more educated approach when dealing with controversial subjects. For instance, the question of ghosts was still one of those things that still had me a little confused. If people are not immortal and don't live on after death, then who are the ghosts? Who are these beings that reportedly visit loved ones or haunt their former dwellings?

This subject was covered during the meetings but I didn't understand how real it was until an interesting encounter. One day I happened to overhear a coworker speaking of his belief in the afterlife. Of course, I could not help but to throw in my two cents about what I was just learning. I guess it didn't really surprise me to learn this man was strongly resistant to any idea that there wasn't an immediate afterlife for the departed. After hearing the story I could understand why he might feel the way he did.

It seems that years earlier this man's uncle had died. This was not just any uncle, but his favorite uncle, the type of uncle that would do anything for you. He told me of how they were very close, so close that they shared many secrets that no one else could possibly know about. Tragically, this favorite uncle died unexpectedly which greatly saddened this nephew. What a void is left in your heart when you lose someone so close. I could relate.

As my coworker told his story he described an event that not only confirmed his view about death, but also gave him great peace. What was the event? Apparently, his uncle came to visit him one evening in his bedroom months after he had died. Yes, in his words this uncle came through his bedroom door into his room and actually sat at the foot of his bed and spoke to him. As this uncle spoke he said things that only the two of them could possibly know. He also told his nephew not to worry about him because he was just fine and happy on the other side. Then the uncle simply got up from the bed, said goodbye and walked back through the door.

I do not recall if he told me he walked through an opened door or a closed one but definitely remember having an eerie feeling as he told this story. I also remember that by the look in this man's eyes, and by the sound of his voice, this guy truly believed what he saw. He was absolutely convinced by what he saw and nobody was going to have success swaying his view. Yes, I believe he saw something. Personally, I do not believe it was the departed soul of his loved one. I did suggest however, that this man might look to the Bible for further study on this subject.

That was an awkward situation to be in. Even though I was beginning to feel very confident in the Bible and my understanding of the state of the dead, I felt a little uncomfortable as to how I should delicately present these truths without offending someone.

How could I tell him that what he saw was not his uncle; especially when it brought him so much comfort? Did it really matter if I shared everything I had learned? Besides, it wouldn't bring his uncle back anyway. Another issue here was the pride that I observed in his voice as he told the story. It was as if he felt special to have been visited by someone beyond the grave. What could I really say? Should I have said anything at all?

Maybe out of compassion for this friend, or maybe it was because I did not yet have full confidence in my beliefs yet that prevented me from getting into this deeper with him. But what I was realizing again was the seriousness and the complexity of issue. Even though no one had ever visited me I knew that this battle was for real! The devil was working very hard to convince people that when you die you don't really die, just as the Bible says. How could Satan use someone like my coworker's uncle to perpetuate his lie? Again, I learned that the Bible explains it clearly.

Let's go back a little to what we talked about in Revelation chapter twelve. Remember, the Bible states that there was war in heaven where Satan and his angels were defeated and cast out of heaven? Where did they end up upon their departure? Yes, earth. Satan and a third of the angels came to earth and began to disrupt God's plan. How? By deceiving the whole world as the Bible says in Revelation 12:9. And I believe he does this through the lie about the state of the dead.

God's word tells us that the devil is like a roaring lion, roaming the earth and seeking those he may devour. Ultimately, his mission is to discredit God and he knows that he has but a short time to do so. But there is more about the ways of this dangerous foe. You see, the Bible tells us that the devil even disguises himself as an angel of light, or truth. Some even believe that he will ultimately impersonate Christ himself in a great last day attempt to deceive the world. Remember the third of the angels that were cast out of heaven? The Bible says that they can also disguise themselves, and even as ministers of truth.

> 2 Corinthians 11:13-15 *For such are false apostles, deceitful workers, transforming themselves into the apostles of Christ. And no marvel; for Satan himself is transformed into an angel of light. Therefore it is no great thing if his ministers also be transformed as the ministers of righteousness; whose end shall be according to their works.*

> Ephesians 6:11,12 *Put on the whole armor of God, that ye may be able to stand against the wiles of the devil. For we wrestle not against flesh and blood, but against principalities, against powers, against the rulers of the darkness of this world, against spiritual wickedness in high places.*

We must understand that Satan will stoop to any level to deceive the world about the character of God and the truth of his word. But why would he use the state of the dead as his primary tool for deception? Here are some thoughts.

1. If the devil can convince us that everyone is immortal then why would we need God, or Jesus as a Savior?
2. If we don't need God then why do we need The Ten Commandments or any other basis for knowing right from wrong?
3. If we are all immortal then why did Jesus have to die?
4. And why would Jesus need to return as he promised?
5. If we don't really die, why should we bother taking care of our bodies?

6. And what would it matter if we don't treat other people with respect?
7. If we are all immortal and don't really need God, then how, and by whom, will we be judged?

The devil knows that if you are confused about the character of God and what really happens at death, then you might just as well throw everything pertaining to a divine moral standard away. In fact, the real issue here is this, if you do not understand the true make up of man and what happens at death then you really cannot understand the true nature or character of God. I realize this is a pretty strong statement to make but I hope you can see the point.

The story I shared about my coworker's uncle is probably just one of thousands, or maybe even millions of like events which have occurred around the world. And all these illusions have the same purpose... to get you to believe in the immortality of the soul. If what the Bible says is true, then while Satan is roaming around the earth like a roaring lion, it makes sense that he hears our conversations, knows our weaknesses, and uses his demon followers to continue his plan of deception. We must remember that he is very powerful and resourceful. Surely if he can impersonate an angel of light then he can appear to a hurting soul as a departed loved one.

I would be remiss here if I did not mention the religions of the world that are either deceived or are being used directly by the devil to perpetuate his lie. Do you personally know of churches or religious systems that pray for, or even worship the souls of the dead? If so, where do you think this practice came from?

If the Bible is true in its straight forward presentation of the death as a sleep, or the final stage of existence prior to the resurrection, then what good can be done by praying for the dead? Here is a very plain scripture that shows that the dead do not even know when they have visitors.

Job 14:21 *His sons come to honour, and he knoweth it not; and they are brought low, but he perceiveth it not.*

What is the purpose of praying for, or to the dead? According to what I have learned from the Bible, there is no purpose for it at all, except that it helps to perpetuate the devil's lie. And you know, in some strange way, maybe the devil actually believes that he is the recipient of those prayers. Or maybe he laughs as he hears the cries of sincere people all over the world pleading that their departed loved ones will not end up in some hellish existence. Or maybe he laughs because he knows that the destiny of everyone is sealed at death. Yes, I believe he laughs. The devils laughs as some pray for God's mercy on the dead, and as others pray to the dead as if they can have some influence in the affairs of men on earth today. Yes, some think that the dead will plead with God on our behalf in hopes that God will be kind to us; as if God needs to be convinced to care about those whom He created.

Some of you may be a little shocked by what you are reading. Or maybe you are just a little stunned by these thoughts just as I was. Let's face it, it's simply hard to comprehend how the whole world could be deceived on this subject. But dear friend, I hope you see how these facts make every day more precious. Instead of living life like we are just passing through on some continuous journey of being perfected or enlightened on our way to obtaining immortality on our own, life is exactly what it is, a gift to be cherished.

As I was learning these things I began to realize how every minute of every day my sensitivity to relationships and purpose became more elevated. When we really know the truth about our lives being little more than a vapor, and how much we are dependant upon God, it truly changes everything. Life was no longer just some temporary situation to me that really didn't matter. Instead, everything was making sense now.

I needed to know that life on earth was important and I now realize that it is. I only wish that I could have known and shared this before Bobby died, or Grandpa, or Aunt Eva, or many of my other relatives and friends. All of these relationships were important, more important than I had ever known. I just wish I could have told them about God's and His love. Maybe their lives could have been more fulfilling. Maybe they could have had a closer walk with God as result of knowing His true character. And more importantly still, there's a good chance this information could have greatly influenced their eternal destiny.

Only God knows the ultimate destiny of every person. Quite frankly, all we can do is speculate and hope. That is, unless we know the truth. Yes, we can hope that the hearts of our loved ones were right with God when they died, but don't you want to be sure? Well we can know without a doubt where every person will end up? The Bible is quite helpful in showing the criteria by which all will be judged as well as where every person will spend eternity.

As we enter deeper into this little book we will discuss some controversial passages that I struggled with. And we will also show how God's love is even revealed in the way He deals with the wicked. For some, these next chapters may be difficult ones to take. But I make you this promise: I will do my best to present what I learned in hopes that it brings you as much peace as it has brought to me.

Chapter 14

Can We Communicate With the Dead?

Through our studies and absorbing everything we could along the way we realized that news like this is not without its critics. For whatever reason, most people are under the impression that you have to be some kind of great theologian or prophet to truly understand the Bible. Honestly, I used to feel the same way, but not anymore. In fact, some of the most skilled Bible experts I know have no special credentials whatsoever. Still, if you don't have some kind of fancy title, most people are not going to listen to what you have to say. It's sort of ironic though when you think about it, the disciples of Jesus were not really considered the cream of the crop either. But look what they did when the Holy Spirit had been granted to them.

One good reason why we should study this subject in depth is because of the fact that the media is such a powerful influence on what we think. If we are not grounded in the truth, it is very likely that we will be deceived through smooth and subtle ways. Hearing stories about visitations from beyond and haunted houses inhabited by ghosts or lost souls sure make for good entertainment. And whether we realize it or not, they can work to shape what we believe.

Just think about the mediums we often hear about who claim to be able to communicate with the dead. How many times do you have to hear about or watch such presentations before you begin to believe they are actually talking to the dead? Recently, I saw a couple on television claiming to have some gift for talking to the dead. I wonder how much money they make. Funny though, I never heard them, or any of the others medium personalities for that matter, mention anything about God. Strange isn't it? I wonder what these people would do for work if the world realized that what they claimed to be doing was impossible. I'm not suggesting that all of these mediums are simply talking to the air in an attempt to capitalize on hurting people, although this may be the case. No, some of them may actually be communicating with something. But I am fully convinced that it is not Uncle Joe or Aunt Betty. Based on what we have learned from the Bible, it's quite clear that this is a practice that should not be entered into.

> Isaiah 8:19,20 *And when they shall say unto you, Seek unto them that have familiar spirits, and unto wizards that peep, and that mutter: should not a people seek unto their God? For the living to the dead? To the law and to the testimony: if they speak not according to this word, it is because there is no light in them.*

For a long time I was not aware of what the Bible says about communicating with the spirit world. What I found is that God strongly condemns the practice in His word. Either the world does not know this fact, or it is disregarding God's warning altogether. But if the world is, in fact, aware that God doesn't want us to embrace mediums and communication with the spirit world, why wouldn't we listen? Is it because many of us have unresolved issues with those who have died? Still, I don't think there is ever a good enough reason to disregard what God says. If He says we shouldn't do something, we should listen.

> **Leviticus 20:6** *And the soul that turneth after such as have familiar spirits, and after wizards, to go a whoring after them, I will even set my face against that soul, and will cut him off from among his people.*

King Saul was someone I learned about when studying this topic. Some today believe that because this king attempted to contact the dead through the use of a medium proves that souls live on after death. But is this really the case?

Reading of the account of events leading up to the death of King Saul show that he was a very desperate man. King Saul had disobeyed God to the point where his heart was hardened. Saul had planned to kill David, among other things, which displeased God. Therefore, God would no longer hear the king's prayers as recorded in 1 Samuel 28:6. But because of the fact that the king was so desperate to know what would come to pass, he again disobeyed by seeking after a witch, a practice that had been condemned by God.

> **1 Samuel 28:6-8** *And when Saul enquired of the Lord, the lord answered him not, neither by dreams, nor by Urim, nor by prophets. Then said Saul unto his servants, Seek me a woman that hath a familiar spirit, that I may go to her, and enquire of her. And his servants said to him, Behold, there is a woman that hath a familiar spirit at Endor. And Saul disguised himself, and put on other raiment, and he went, and two men with him, and they came to the woman by night: and he said, I pray thee divine unto me by the*

familiar spirit, and bring me him up, whom I shall name unto thee.

Not only did Saul know that he was on shaky ground here by disguising himself and visiting the witch at night, but he also got quite the reminder from the witch that the practice had been forbidden by the king himself, and the penalty for the practice was death, verse 9. But the disguised king assured the woman that nothing would happen to her, verse 10. And notice where the spirit was to be conjured from. Here's a tip... it was not from above.

1 Samuel 28:11-13 Then said the woman, Whom shall I bring up unto thee? And he said, Bring me up Samuel. And when the woman saw Samuel, she cried with a loud voice: and the woman spake to Saul, Saying, why has thou deceived me? For thou art Saul. And the king said unto her, Be not afraid: for what sawest thou? And the woman saith unto Saul, I saw gods ascending out of the earth.

So, here we find a couple of interesting points. First, Saul must have known enough about those who have died to understand they were not in heaven. This is because he asked the witch to bring him up. Secondly, the woman said she saw gods ascending out the earth. Notice she was not seeing the God of heaven. So what kind of spirits do you think she was conjuring up here? Let's read on...

1 Samuel 28:14,15 And he said unto her, What form is he of? And she said, An old man cometh up: and he is covered with as mantel. And Saul perceived that it was Samuel, and he stooped with his face to the ground, and bowed himself. And Samuel said to Saul, Why hast thou disquieted me? to bring me up? And

> *Saul answered, I am sore distressed; for the Philistines make war against me, and God is departed from me, and answereth me no more, neither by prophet, nor by dreams: therefore I have called thee, that thou mayest make known unto me what I shall do.*

If this were really a passage that proved the souls lives on after death then where did Samuel get the body of an old man? And what is the mantel all about? Interesting isn't it?

As I read further I was convinced this is very dangerous stuff because in the next few lines I detected words that sounded an awful lot like they came straight from the mouth of the devil himself as he realized what an opportunity he had before him. To me anyway, these words came strangely close to what the serpent said to Eve in the garden.

> *1 Samuel 28:16-20 Then said Samuel, Wherefore then dost thou ask of me, seeing the Lord is departed from thee, and is become thine enemy? And the Lord hath done to him, as he spake by me: for the Lord hath rent the kingdom out of thine hand, and given it to thy neighbor, even to David. Because thou obeyedst not the voice of the Lord, nor executedst his fierce wrath upon Amalek, therefore hath the Lord done this thing to thee this day. Moreover the Lord will also deliver Israel with thee into the hand of the Philistines: and to morrow shalt thou and thy sons be with me: the Lord also shall deliver the host of Israel into the hand of the Philistines. Then Saul fell straightway all along on the earth, and was sore afraid, because of the words of Samuel: and there was no strength in him; for he had eaten no bread all day, nor all the night.*

Notice that Saul did not actually see the spirit because he asked the witch to describe how this so-called Samuel appeared to her. However, the perceived spirit gave the king a gloom and doom message that served as a self fulfilling prophecy. As Saul accepted the spirit from the earth's condemning words, the king's demeanor served to seal his fate, and that of his sons. But don't miss this, after telling Saul that he would lose his kingdom and his life because of his disobedience, the spirit told the king that he and his sons would be with him.

This brings up a question. Wasn't Samuel a prophet of God? If so, wouldn't he be in heaven if people really went there upon death? Not only does the idea that the disobedient king would be joining the prophet not make any sense, but Samuel was said to have come from the earth to begin with. Maybe you can see how confusing, and dangerous all of this is. Yes, unfortunately, Saul was an example why you should not shun God, nor seek those with familiar spirits.

As I was studying this topic I learned that belief in the immortality of the soul and the afterlife has become a large part of many of the world's religions. In fact, most pagan or non-Christian religions are strongly based on belief in the spirit world. Even the Christian faiths have embraced the afterlife, or immortality of the soul as a commonly held belief. Maybe they are completely unaware that Satan has been instrumental in the merging of paganism and spiritualism into Christianity. I would surely hope that they understand the history of the church. And I would hope they understand that after Satan unsuccessfully attempted to destroy the church by killing millions of martyrs, he decided to work from within. Do they?

Many people simply believe in the immortality of the soul because it just may be the only thing that gives them hope, hope for their loved ones and hope for themselves. But what is that hope really based on? Do they hope that the dead float around somewhere completely out of sight after these bodies wear out, and you have to use some medium to contact them? Sorry but that idea doesn't bring me much hope. From what I have learned through this journey, God is much, much smarter than that. Surely He has more for us than to simply have us flounder around in some state of transparent meaningless existence as we wait for everyone else.

If communicating with the dead were even possible, I find it hard to believe that God would have us struggle to do so. Surely if it were possible then He could come up with a better way to make contact. Having departed souls knock on walls or spooking people by lurking in the shadows surely can't serve any great purpose. No, scaring people is the devil's job.

Here's a good question for those who believe in immortal souls and ghosts: Why is it that only some of the souls of the dead attempt to communicate with the living? Are there only a few ghosts that have that special privilege? It seems to me that if your earthly status had anything to do with it then George Washington or Abe Lincoln, or Ben Franklin, or even Mother Teresa would be at the head of the line, ready and anxious to communicate with the world. Who knows, maybe Ben Franklin or Thomas Edison are inventing something right now to communicate with us. Couldn't we use their help about now?

Wouldn't it be great if someone very wise like King Solomon could give the leaders of the world some advice? I know it sounds like I am making fun here but if the souls of the dead are out there somewhere, wouldn't it make sense that God would want them to help us? Sure He would. But sadly, there has not been a peep from any of these great people. We have to ask ourselves why that is.

I have also wondered why it is that those who have "passed" seem to communicate only with those who claim to have some sort of gift. Since God condemns the practice then they must have gotten this gift from someone else. Hmmm. I might be wrong here but I can't help but to believe that if God created all of us then he would use Christians as His mediums. Another interesting thought is that many Christian leaders teach that since we are made in the image of God, we are spirits just as God is a spirit. Okay, if we are, then why can't we easily communicate with the spirit world? Is it because something magical happens when we die which triggers some new dimension that gives us the ability to talk to other spirits? Sorry, but I just don't believe it. And Bible doesn't teach it either.

We must not be deceived by all of the confusion relating to the state of the dead. All we have to do is remember the lie, the first lie. This should be our first clue as to what is really going on here. And we must know what the Bible says about the dead being asleep and not knowing anything. Even though we are being bombarded with an ever-increasing flood of books, movies and television programs exploring and supporting the first lie, we are much too smart to be fooled. Aren't we?

> 1 Timothy 4:1 *Now the Spirit speaketh expressly, that in the latter times some shall depart from the faith, giving heed to seducing spirits, and doctrines of devils...*

If there are voices and noises that people have heard, they are not coming from the dead, but the living. Yes, the living, fallen angels who are working hard to serve their master. Demons are real! And we can look to the Bible to see that the devil will use both ghostly impersonations and even demons to possess humans.

> Matthew 8: 28,29 *And when he was come to the other side into the country of the Gergenes, there met him two possessed with devils, coming out of the tombs, exceeding fierce, so that no man might pass that way. And behold, they cried out, saying, what have we to*

do with thee, Jesus, thou Son of God? Art thou come hither to torment us before the time?

The story goes on to say that Jesus cast out the demons into a herd of swine. But I want you to notice two things here in addition to the fact that demons will take possession of humans. The first is that these demons were fully aware of who Jesus was. Secondly, and don't miss this, they asked Jesus if he had come to torment them <u>before the time</u>. Yes, they also knew that there would come a time of judgment for the devil and all of his followers.

The Bible tells us of an increase in spiritual activity in the last days just before the <u>time</u> spoken of by these demons. Again, the devil knows that he has but a short time to deceive as many as he can. His deceptions are designed to take the attention off of God and the salvation offered through His Son and make people think that there is power in partnering with the forces of darkness. Oh there is power alright, but be warned. You don't want to mess around with this evil power. Because even though we may think it will get us somewhere, it's not the place where we will want to go. Jesus is the only way that humans can have eternal life and the devil knows it. Therefore, don't waste your time attempting to communicate with the dead. Communicate with the Living God instead!

Chapter 15

Don't Some Text Teach An Immediate Reward?

*E*ven though there is overwhelming evidence to the contrary, I have heard many Christian leaders use a few choice scriptures to attempt to justify their belief in an immediate reward at death. These ministers would say things like, "absent from the body, present with the Lord." Some use parables and stories that Jesus told to make their case. For instance, many used the story of the rich man and Lazarus, or the story of the thief on the cross as the basis for their argument. But do these passages really prove the immortality of the soul or instant paradise?

Here are a few passages of scriptures I looked up to see if they can be used to overturn the overwhelming evidence to the contrary. See what you think. First, does Paul's statement about being absent from the body and present with the Lord prove that a person goes to heaven immediately upon death? I once thought so.

2 Corinthians 4:16-5:10 *For which cause (the cause of Christ) we faint not; but though our outward man*

perish, yet the inward man is renewed day by day. For our light affliction, which is but for a moment, worketh for us a far more exceeding and eternal weight of glory; While we look not at the things which are seen, but at the things which are not seen: for the things which are seem are temporal; but the things which are not seen are eternal. For we know that if our earthly house of this tabernacle were dissolved, we have a building of God, an house not made with hands, eternal in the heavens. For in this we groan, earnestly desiring to be clothed upon with our house which is from heaven: If so be that being clothed we shall not be found naked. For we that are in this tabernacle do groan, being burdened: not for that we would be unclothed, but clothed upon, that mortality might be swallowed up of life.

Before we move on here I want to point out some things that you may already realize. In the first place, the King James Version can often be difficult to understand. Secondly, Paul is speaking of the body here. As we get older our bodies wear out and we often groan about that. They often burden us and plague us and Paul was attempting to persuade his listeners that they should not get too hung up on the things of the flesh, but focus instead on spiritual things. Lets read on from 2 Corinthians 5:5.

Now he that hath wrought us for the selfsame thing is God, who also hath given unto us the earnest of the Spirit. Therefore we are always confident, knowing that whilst we are at home in the body, we are absent from the Lord: For we walk by faith and not by sight: We are confident, I say, and willing rather to be absent from the body, and to be present with the Lord. Wherefore we labour, that, whether present or absent, we may be accepted of him. For we must all appear before the judgment seat of Christ; that every one may receive the things done in the body, according to that he hath done, whether it be good or bad.

I will move ahead here just a bit so that we can get the full context of what Paul was talking about. This is in the same chapter.

2 Corinthians 5:16,17 *Wherefore henceforth know we no man after the flesh; yea, though we have known Christ after the flesh, yet now henceforth know we him no more. Therefore if any man be in Christ, he is a new creature: old things are passed away; behold, all things are become new.*

Was Paul talking about what happens to a person when they die here? Was there any mention of an immortal soul? Of course not. Paul was simply telling believers things had changed and that they should not get too comfortable or concerned with things of the flesh. In addition, Paul was essentially saying that whether in the body, or in tune with Christ by the power of the Spirit, they were to labor to be acceptable to God because all would be judged based on what they did in the body.

It's understandable why a passage like the one above can be used to justify a person's belief. In fact, it was an elderly friend from work who sprung this one on me. I respect this elder gentleman and remember him as being one of the most loving and thoughtful Christians I have ever known. Cal is his name and I know that he really loves Jesus. His greatest hope was to be with Jesus some day and I could never say that he won't realize that dream. However, the point is not *if* he will someday be with the Lord, but *when* and *how* that will actually happen. To my friend, or even with the apostle

Paul, from the time they fall into that unconscious sleep until they see Jesus at the resurrection, the time lapse will be as if it is but the twinkling of the eye.

One more important point about this present with the Lord belief is the fact that Paul tells us in 2 Corinthians 5 that mortals will "put on immortality" when Christ comes the second time. Obviously, this clearly reiterates the Bible teaching that humans are not immortal in their current state only to be translated at death. No, immortality will be given as a gift "at the last trump" when Jesus returns. Therefore, I had to admit that there was simply not enough evidence here to overturn all of the other Bible passages about the dead being in their graves.

Another passage that is used by many to prove an immediate reward can also be confusing because on the surface it seems to present the idea that the dead can talk to each other. But did Jesus actually contradict the Bible? Or, was he simply using this story to illustrate a point about the finality of death. When we read this passage we must understand that this story was part of a collection of parables or stories that Jesus was telling to many publicans, sinners, and his disciples. The use of the term "a certain rich man" in this passage is a strong indicator that this is, in fact, a parable used to illustrate a greater truth.

> Luke 16:19-31 *There was a certain rich man, which was clothed in purple and fine linen, and fared sumptuously every day. And there was a certain beggar named Lazarus, which was laid at his gate, full of sores, And desiring to be fed with the crumbs which fell from the rich man's table: moreover the dogs came and licked his sores. And it came to pass, that the beggar died, and was carried by the angels to Abraham's bosom: the rich man also died, and was buried; And in hell he lift up his eyes, being in*

torments, and seeth Abraham far off, and Lazarus in his bosom. And he cried and said, Father Abraham, have mercy on me, and send Lazarus, that he may dip the tip of his finger in water, and cool my tongue; for I am tormented in this flame. But Abraham said, Son, remember that thou in thy lifetime receivedst thy good things, and likewise Lazarus evil things: but now he is comforted, and thou art tormented. And beside all this, between us and you there is a great gulf fixed: so that they which would pass from hence to you cannot; neither can they pass to us, that would come from thence. Then he said, I pray thee therefore, father, that thou wouldest send him to my father's house: For I have five brethren; that he may testify unto them, lest they also come into this place of torment. Abraham saith unto him, They have Moses and the prophets; let them hear them. And he said, Nay, father Abraham: but if one went unto them from the dead, they will repent. And he said unto him, If they hear not Moses and the prophets, neither will they be persuaded, though one rose from the dead.

    This was another tough one for me. You see, a very good Christian friend of mine used this passage in an attempt to show that the dead are not asleep. And to be honest I had to take a real hard look at this story to make it fit with the rest of the Bible. However, what I found was quite amazing. The story did not conflict with the other passages at all. But it simply took some effort to see it.
    When you use scripture to understand scripture, we can easily see that the idea that the dead are able to communicate across an abyss starkly conflicts with what we read in Ecclesiastes 9:5, "the dead know not anything." Therefore, this clearly shows that we should not take this passage literally, but symbolically. This, coupled with the fact that our

reward does not come until the second coming, proves again that this must be understood symbolically.

Jesus was making many points in this story. First, he wanted the people to know that when you have been given much you should have mercy on those less fortunate. Secondly, once your destiny is sealed, there is no second chance or deal making to help your family. Thirdly, there will be no travel between the fixed gulf between hell, (the grave) and heaven.

As far as the place of torment is concerned, the Bible teaches that the wicked will be tormented with guilt and destroyed by fire. In this passage Jesus was most likely covering all of the feelings and emotions of the wicked who will receive their reward at the second death. We will talk more about that later.

It is also interesting to me that this rich man was pleading to Abraham. Obviously, this message was intended for the Jews who held Abraham in high esteem. However, Abraham is not God and therefore not in charge of who goes where. But my question was: where was Abraham? Was he actually in heaven? The answer is found in this exchange between the Pharisees and Jesus as recorded in the book of John.

> John 8:51 *Verily, verily I say unto you, If a man keep my saying, he shall never see death. Then said the Jews unto him, Now we know that thou hast a devil.* <u>Abraham is dead.</u> *, and the prophets; and thou sayest. If a man keep my saying, he shall never taste of death. Art thou greater than our father Abraham, which is dead? and the prophets are dead: whom makest thou thyself? Jesus answered, If I honour myself, my honour is nothing: it is my Father that honoureth me; of whom ye say, that he is your God: Yet ye have not known him; but I know him: and if I should say, I know him not, I shall be a liar like unto*

you: but I know him, and keep his saying. Your father Abraham rejoiced to see my day: and he saw it, and was glad. Then said the Jews unto him, Thou are not yet fifty years old, and hast thou seen Abraham? Jesus said unto them, Verily, verily, I say unto you, Before Abraham was, I am. Then took they up stones to cast at him:

Notice that Jesus did not say anything about Abraham being in heaven. And even the Jews knew that Abraham and the prophets were dead as they doubted the words of Jesus about how Abraham could have seen Jesus' day. But just so there is no question regarding the current place of those like Abraham who had close walks with God, I reviewed what I had read about King David. If you recall, David was *a man of God's own heart*. Surely, if anyone would be in heaven it would be him, right?

Acts 2:29, 34 *Men and brethren, let me freely speak unto you of the patriarch David, that he is both dead and buried, and his sepulcher is with us unto this day. 34 For David is not ascended into the heavens:*

With the overwhelming evidence I had been shown about death being a sleep until Jesus comes, each difficult text presented could be made to fit. Are there others? Yes. In fact, we will look at possibly the most controversial of them all in the next chapter. However, not every potentially contrary text is being presented in this book. Be aware, you will have people try to show you one or two text that seem to teach that the soul is immortal. But don't buy it. Make them prove it by making all the scriptures fit. From my experience, they won't be able to do it.

Here is a tip... whenever you have a passage of scripture that seems to contradict a majority of the Bible, remember who it is that wants you to be confused. Yes, it is Satan. The false teaching about the immortality of the soul has caused nothing but confusion and mysterious wonder which are contrary to plain Bible teachings. But God has shown us very clearly that when you accept His way, there is nothing but absolutely logical answers which prove His love and fairness.

Chapter 16

What About the Promise to the Thief?

*M*aybe the most popular story in the Bible for justifying the belief in an immediate reward after death is the story of the thief on the cross. But does this passage really prove an immediate reward? Didn't Jesus tell the thief that he would be with him in paradise *today*? I'm sure many of you have heard the story. But just as a refresher, let's read part of it again. The story is found in Luke chapter twenty-three. We will focus in on verses thirty-eight to forty-three.

> *And a superscription also was written over him in letters of Greek, and in Latin, and Hebrew, THIS IS THE KING OF THE JEWS. And one of the malefactors which were hanged railed on him, saying If thou be Christ, save thyself and us. But the other answering rebuked him, saying Dost thou not fear God, seeing thou art in the same condemnation? And we indeed justly; for we receive the true reward of our deeds: but this man hath done nothing amiss. And he said unto Jesus, Lord, remember me when*

thou comest into thy kingdom. And Jesus said unto him, <u>Verily I say unto thee, today shalt thou be with me in paradise.</u>

When I first heard that this was one of the passages that contradicted what we were learning, I could easily see why. In his response to the thief who recognized Jesus for who he truly was, the Savior seemed to make it clear that the thief would receive his reward that day. But did the words of Jesus actually disprove death being a sleep until the resurrection? Had the Bible contradicted itself? To be honest, we needed help with this one.

It was explained to us that if you look at this passage carefully and logically, considering the full context, there was no conflict whatsoever. One of the first things to consider here is the fact that Jesus could not have possibly promised the man they would be together that day. Why? This is because Jesus himself had not gone to paradise, or heaven, yet. You see, even though it is clear that Jesus died shortly after that promise to the thief, He did not rise from the tomb until the third day. And, if there is any question about where He was for those three days, the question can be quickly answered when we read the account of His conversation with Mary Magdalene shortly after his resurrection.

John 20:11-17 But Mary stood without at the sepulcher weeping: and as she wept, she stooped down, and looked into the sepulcher, And seeth two angels in white sitting, the one at the head and the other at the feet, where the body of Jesus had lain. And they say unto her, Woman, why weepest thou? She saith unto them, Because they have taken away my Lord, and I know not where they have laid him. And when she had thus said, she turned herself back, and saw Jesus standing, and knew not that it was Jesus. Jesus *saith unto her, Woman, why weepest thou? Whom seekest thou? She, supposing him to be the gardener, saith unto him, Sir, if thou have borne him hence, tell me where thou hast laid him, and I will take him away. Jesus saith unto her, Mary, She turned herself, and saith unto him, Rabboni; which is to say Master. Jesus saith unto her, <u>Touch me not; for I am not yet ascended to my Father</u>: but go to my brethren, and say unto them, I ascend unto my Father, and your Father; and to my God, and your God.*

Obviously, Jesus had no reason to lie to one of His most devoted followers. He simply and plainly told Mary that He had not yet ascended to His Father. This conversation happened days after Jesus had spoken to the thief hanging next to him on the cross.

So what was Jesus really saying when he spoke to the repentant thief? Was the thief going somewhere else; somewhere that may be sort of the opposite of purgatory? This next passage got us closer to the truth.

John 19:31-33 The Jews therefore, because it was the preparation, that the bodies should not remain upon the cross on the sabbath day, (for that sabbath day was an high day,) besought Pilate that their legs might be broken, and that they might be taken away. Then came the soldiers, and brake the legs of the first, and of the other which was crucified with him. But when they came to Jesus, and saw that he was dead already, they brake not his legs:

Because of the fact that the Romans honored the Jews by taking bodies down on the special Sabbath, but would break the legs of only those who were still alive so they could not run away, they did not have to break the legs of

Jesus. This was because He was dead already. Therefore, in this account, there is no reason to believe that the thief died that day either. In fact, the evening quickly came upon them as sundown marked a new day.

Many people do not know that when God created a day, the evening was the first part. Yes, the Bible states that *the evening and the morning were the first day.* Genesis 1:5. And, you might recall the fact that even the Jewish people today still hold to that standard as their days are counted with a new day starting when the sun goes down.

Now we have two fairly convincing contradictions to the idea that the thief went to heaven that day. First we know that Jesus himself had not ascended on the day of the supposed promise. Then we have the issue of doubt about the thief not being dead on the day in question. So how do we figure this one out? The answer is so simple that you will probably laugh, but maybe even cry when you begin to realize how much of the world has been misled on this subject.

The issue all comes down to the punctuation. That's right. Even though the Bible teaches that all of the *original* scriptures were recorded by men under inspiration from the Holy Spirit, the punctuation was added later. Therefore, it is not only possible, but likely that when the punctuation was added to the text, it was not inspired. Instead, the punctuation was placed by editors who based the positioning on their own understanding or interpretation of the text at the time.

Can the punctuation really make that much of a difference? Sure it can. Maybe you remember the story about someone writing a note on a blackboard at school while the teacher was out of the room. The note on the blackboard read… Johnny said the teacher is an idiot. When the teacher came into the room and saw the note on the board, stared at it for a moment, then picked up the chalk and made a slight modification in the sentence which brought out quite a laugh from the class. The teacher simply added two commas. Now the sentence read…

Questioning Death

Johnny, said the teacher, is an idiot. I think you get the point. So, let's read the text in Luke again. But this time, we will simply move one of the commas over a bit.

John 23:43 **Before** *And Jesus said unto him, Verily I say unto thee, today shalt thou be with me in paradise.*

John 23:43 **After** *And Jesus said unto him, Verily I say unto thee today, shalt thou be with me in paradise.*

By simply moving a comma or removing it altogether, you can completely alter the meaning of any sentence. With this in mind we could clearly see there was no reason to believe the Bible contradicted itself. In fact, I was pretty amazed how well it was all fitting together.

This very important and potentially crippling text could have undermined everything we had learned. But again, the overriding truth prevailed. Neither Jesus, nor the thief went to Heaven that day. Jesus did, however, promise the repentant thief that when He did eventually come into His kingdom, at the time appointed by His Father, the thief would be among those to be raised and brought into paradise. Yes, Jesus could assure the thief that upon returning at His second coming, all those who believed in Him would be resurrected and taken to heaven. What a promise for the thief. What a hope for us! Maybe you are thinking the same thing right now but I simply could not get over the fact that no one had ever told me this stuff before. Here I was in my thirties and I was learning something that seemed so simple and clear. It was hard for me, and Karen as well, to understand why this was not common knowledge, especially among church-goers.

I hope you can see why believing that the souls of the dead go to heaven or hell immediately at death just did not make any sense. And for anyone that believes this, please consider this question. For a person whom died four thousand years ago, what sense would it make to be in heaven for so long and only to have to come back for their body thousands of years later? It seems to me that it's no different if someone is supposedly taken up in some secret event, like a rapture. Why come back for your body later? Now do you see how much the devil has messed things up?

Some of you may be quite astonished at what you are reading. That is perfectly understandable. I was too. Some might be a least a little angry as well, or maybe even mad at me. That's okay. Whatever you do, please don't make the mistake of being angry with God. The truth has been there all along. It's the devil who deserves our anger. Of course, this is easy for me to say now. But please know that I sympathize with many of you who are realizing for the first time that the wool has been pulled over your eyes, and that a strong possibility exists that you have believed a lie for all these years.

Sometimes we learn things that are hard to accept, especially when we have believed a certain way for so long. But God's way is really the best. And as we dig still deeper, you will see the perfection of His entire plan. So stay with me.

Chapter 17

Would A Loving God Torment People Forever?

The personal Bible studies and the seminar meetings were certainly a blessing to both Karen and I. But what really made this more than just new information that was giving me peace of mind happened on my way to work one morning. You see, I had been struggling to give up smoking and drinking. And the more we had learned about everything God had done for us, the more I wanted to quit these terrible habits. Yes, I wanted to quit so bad it hurt, both emotionally and physically. While driving in my car and attempting to fight the urge to reach under the car seat for my stash of cigarettes, the tears began to flow. These little poisonous cancer sticks had me and for the first time I would have to admit it. I felt so bad about not being able to stop on my own, along with the fact that I'd been lying to my wife, that it moved me to I cry out to God for help. "I can't do this on my own. Please, Lord, help me!"

Guess what happened. The urges were gone! And you know what else? It was the first time in my life that I knew for sure that God loved me. Yes, me! And this was not because I was a good person or anything like that. He always loved me. It just never felt it like I did that day. But it also did something else for me. This experience was like a pat on the back from God that told me I was on the right track. And although the devil was working hard during that period, the experience was like being born again. It gave me new wind in my sails as if I was just learning how to walk and my dad was just a few feet away encouraging me to keep going. And because of that day, I will keep going, and I want others to keep going as well. God is Love, friend. And He is also just.

Sorry for getting sidetracked but I just really want you to understand where I am coming from in all of this. My experiences in coming to these conclusions are really not just from books. This is my life! And if you knew just how bad of a typist I was, you would know how I struggled to get every word down and how serious I am about setting the record straight. Quite frankly, I love God, and I HATE what the devil has done!

Because God knows death means separation from Him, He made a plan for us to be reconciled back into a relationship with Him. He wants to be with you, friend, and with me. The Bible tells us that God is not willing that any would perish, but that all would come to repentance. I want you to notice the word perish in the last statement. Do you remember that word from anywhere in the Bible? You got it. John 3:16 says…

> *For God so loved the world, that he gave his only begotten Son, that whosoever believeth in him shall not perish, but have everlasting life.*

And now as we get into some deeper issues I need you to remember that word, *perish*. It is very important. But there's something else I would ask you to think about and remember that we just read in the passage above. It is the term *everlasting life*. What do you think the exact opposite of everlasting life is? Think about it hard before you answer. The exact opposite of everlasting life is... everlasting death, or just plain death! Don't the terms perish, and everlasting death, mean the same thing? Here is something else to consider... the exact opposite of *everlasting life* is <u>not</u> *everlasting torment*, or *eternal torment*.

This may be shocking to a few people right now but you need to understand the above points. Why? Because it is very difficult to accept the fact that God is a God of love if you believe that He would eternally torment people. I must say that I had difficulty reconciling this contradiction in my mind. That is, until I was shown the truth about the character of God, death, and the devil's plan.

When God made the heavens and the earth and all of the creatures, He gave those with the ability to reason the right to choose. Because when you really think about it, loving someone means you give them the right to say yes, or no. When Lucifer made his choice to rebel because of his discontent and jealousy, he was able to deceive others to follow him. Because of his beauty and status in the ranks of heaven he used his influence to convince a third of the angels that God was a controlling tyrant. His reasoning was that God was unfair in requiring obedience to Himself, and that all creatures should be able to do whatever they want and still receive the blessings of heaven. Lucifer accused God of buying the obedience of the others, and if they were not all programmed to obey, they too would not honor Him.

We can also see what has happened as a result of second guessing the Creator's authority and wisdom. God knows the beginning from the end and knows what happens when beings are not content with what they have been given. When one feels like they are entitled to more and do not appreciate what they have, sin is the result. In the same way that Satan's pride got the best of him, God knows that the best path to order is obedience. However, if one selfishly decides to go their own way, God will not stop them. He is not only a God of mercy, but one of love as well. And because of this, God will not allow wickedness to go on forever. Eventually, He will put and end to sin and suffering.

In this great battle and ultimately in the final judgment, it is actually God who is being judged. Yes, the entire universe is watching to see what happens in this conflict. While Satan continues his attack on God's character and plan, we must decide. Was Satan right? Or is God right and deserving of our allegiance? Personally, I believe that law and order are the best way. Our Heavenly Father is much smarter than we are and without some kind of order, only chaos can result. Within each of us God has created a conscience that gives us the ability to know right from wrong. But He will not force us to choose Him. However, God knows that when we truly see the result of lawlessness and rebellion, then we will make the right choice.

The devil's heart has been hardened by sin. And we all know the old saying that misery loves company. Satan used a medium as a puppet to twist God's words in the garden and he still uses whatever he can today to draw people from obedience to the Creator. Whether it is God's word, the media, or individual men and women, Satan's greatest desire is to take as many down as possible. This is because he knows he has but a short time. Rev 12:12.

Just as God understands that death can permanently separate us from Him and has made provision for us to live again, the devil also knows that death is bad. And he is doing everything he can to make us think that death is not bad. Or, better yet, he wants us to believe that we don't really die at all. But here is the twist: if the devil can convince us that we don't really die, then he can deceive people into thinking that God will torture people forever.

It is so sad to listen to hellfire and brimstone preachers who use eternal torment in an attempt to scare people into the arms of Jesus. Don't they see the contradiction? Don't they know that to scare a person into accepting God gives them an empty form of faith? Do they really need to resort to scare tactics? How any preacher who really knows the love of God as displayed at the cross could ever come to such a conclusion, I will never know. Do we really want people to come to Jesus out of fear, like God will burn us forever if we don't? What kind of relationship would that be?

People should be taught to love God because He is truly a God of love and not because he will burn them forever if they don't. The fact is, those who choose to be rebellious and wicked will receive their reward, and it will not be a pleasant reward. However, even though it may be hard to understand, God's love is even displayed in the fact that the wicked will be destroyed quickly. You see, it is the devil that deceives people into thinking that God will torture people for ever and ever.

To expose this lie, here are just a few clear examples of what happens to the wicked. These passages not only describe when the wicked will receive their reward, but what will be left.

> Malachi 4:1 *For, behold the day cometh, that shall burn as an oven; and all the proud, yea, and all that do wickedly, shall be <u>stubble</u>: and the day that cometh shall burn them up, saith the Lord of hosts, that it shall leave them neither root nor branch.*

> Matthew 25:41 *Then shall he also say unto them on the left hand, Depart from me, ye cursed, into everlasting fire, <u>prepared for the devil and his angels</u>:*

Jude 7 *Even as Sodom and Gomorrha, and the cities about them in like manner, giving themselves over to fornication, and going after strange flesh, are set forth for an example, suffering the vengeance of <u>eternal fire</u>.*

2 Peter 2:6 *And turning the cities of Sodom and Gomorrha into <u>ashes</u> condemned them with an overthrow, making them an ensample unto those that after should live ungodly.*

2 Peter 3:7 *But the heavens and the earth, which are now, by the same word are kept in store, reserved unto fire against the <u>day of judgment</u> and perdition of ungodly men.*

Revelation 14:11 *And the smoke of their torment ascendeth up for ever and ever:*

Psalm 37:20 *And the wicked shall perish, and the enemies of the Lord shall be as the fat of lambs: they shall consume; into smoke shall they consume away.*

 The truth about the ultimate fate of the wicked is clear. Eternal torment is simply not what God is all about. Will the wicked be destroyed? Yes. Are there people burning now? No. Will the wicked be punished forever? Sorry, that's not going to happen either. Just because the fire is everlasting or eternal does not mean that the punishment is. I have looked at this from every angle and I just don't find any proof of eternal torment. And, I also don't believe that God would expect anybody to come to Him if He were going to burn people forever. Even the wicked!
 Those who choose the way of the flesh will simply be destroyed on the Day of Judgment. Neither root nor branch

will be left. It's not the punishment that will go on forever, but the smoke of the fire that continues to rise. You see, Sodom and Gomorrha were burned with everlasting fire but they are not still burning today! This is a great example of why eternal or everlasting fire does not make the punishment eternal. Think of it this way, if the wicked really did burn forever as some believe, wouldn't that make them immortal? Again we can see the devil's lie in action.

Another thing that came up while studying this issue was the idea that God and the devil were somehow in this thing together; as if the good people will go to heaven immediately at death, and the bad people will go to hell immediately at their death. And then, in some strange twist, the devil seems to be the one in charge of hell with a pitch fork and the red suit. But how or why would God allow such a thing? He wouldn't. I hope you see how crazy all of this is!

Did you know that the word hell, or hades, simply means the grave or the place of the dead? The idea of a hell as a place of eternal torment is an invention of the devil that has been superstitiously handed down from Paganism to Christianity. Again, this flies in the face of the loving character of God.

I am sharing some pretty strong feelings about the devil's lies because at the time I learned them it made me pretty angry. The more I learned about God and Jesus, the more I was shocked to see how the devil was twisting everything and even more shocked as I realized that many, often sincere preachers who claim to have knowledge of God perpetuate the devil's lies.

How can it be that so many have taken the devil's bait? I would be the first to admit that I'm not the smartest guy in the world but come on! Either the Bible is the true word of God or it isn't. It is upsetting to hear what was coming out of the mouths of those who have a responsibility to preach the truth! But then I realized just what a magnificent job Satan has done in deceiving the whole world.

I will admit this subject can be very confusing. That is, until you realize how the truth has gotten derailed. Keeping this in mind helped me to stay focused in understanding the truth. Believing that God is both loving, and hateful, meant I would have to believe that the devil was the same. But that's where the confusion comes in. We simply have to judge each one fairly based on the best evidence we can find. Therefore, if a person is confused about the character of God, there is little hope that they can, nor would they really want to, understand spiritual things. And the devil knows this so well.

Some might wonder why, if God is love, He allowed Jesus to die. And if Jesus was separated from God because the sins of the world were laid upon Him, wouldn't he have to suffer the fate of the wicked in hell to atone for our sins? I wondered about these issues as well but came to an obvious conclusion. Regarding the question of Jesus going to hell, I had never heard or read of any reports of scars from hellfire on the body of Jesus when He was resurrected. Nor did He use this experience to warn people about what it was like. Therefore, logic tells me that His dying and being in the grave while bearing the sins of the world, and being cast into a burning hell, cannot be one in the same. This means atoning for the sins of the world must involve something else besides experiencing hellfire for sinners. No, the atoning for our sins was achieved through the agony He suffered in the garden and on the cross, coupled with His overcoming death. I believe this is very clear when you look at all of the evidence. What is also clear is that a place of eternal torment does not exist.

So why did Jesus die? How could a God of love allow such a thing? The answer once again is found in the fact that God loved the world so much that He made a plan to give part of Himself that we may be in communion with Him once again. In this plan, Jesus would take upon Himself the sins of the entire world. You see, Jesus not only came to show us how we should treat each other and be obedient to the Father, but also died our death.

> Isaiah 53:5,6,12 *But he was wounded for our transgressions, he was bruised for our iniquities: the chastisement of our peace was upon him; and with his stripes we are healed. All we like sheep have gone astray; we have turned every one to his own way; and the Lord hath laid on him the iniquity of us all. (12) Therefore will I divide him a portion with the great, and he shall divide the spoil with the strong; because he hath poured out his soul unto death: and he was numbered with the transgressors; and he bare the sin of many, and made intercession for the transgressors.*

Quite simply, something had to be done to atone for those sins which would prove to separate man from God for eternity. And Jesus did what had to be done. This means that although a person might experience what is known as the first death, those who had put their faith in the Savior and His sacrifice would not experience the second death. But this isn't quite the whole story. The passion and depth of God's love for you and me is actually revealed quite specifically in what happened to Jesus in the garden of Gethsemane prior to His Crucifixion. Although seemingly reluctant for only a moment, Jesus showed that even during this time of weakness, when He was actually beginning to die, His love for mankind was more powerful than His temporary request for pardon. He knew that failure to follow through with the Father's plan would leave humanity in a hopeless state.

> Matthew 26:38, 39 *Then saith he unto them, My soul is exceeding sorrowful, even unto death: tarry ye here, and watch with me. And he went a little farther and fell on his face, and prayed, saying, O my Father,*

if it be possible, let this cup pass from me: nevertheless not as I will, but as thou wilt.

Even on the cross, Jesus was still feeling the separation from God while experiencing the second death for all who would put their trust in Him. Surely the weight of the world's sins was upon His shoulders. But His love was stronger than death.

Matthew 27:46 *...My God, my God, why hast thou forsaken me?*

It was amazing when I took the time to contemplate what Jesus had done for me. There was just no possible way that I could believe God would burn even the worst of sinners forever. He is simply too merciful and kind. If unrepentant sinners cannot stand before a holy and just Creator when all is said and done, it will not be because He had not given them every opportunity to see the truth and turn from their ways. However, true justice must involve punishment as well as mercy. But come on, eternal torment from a God that would do all of this for me?

Romans 3:24-26 *Being justified freely by his grace through the redemption that is in Christ Jesus: Whom God hath set forth to be a propitiation through faith in his blood, to declare his righteousness for the remission of sins that are past, through the forbearance of God; To declare, I say, at this time his righteousness: that he might be just, and the justifier of him which believeth in Jesus.*

Chapter 18

When Will the Church Be Raptured?

During the period of time while Karen and I were growing in our knowledge, we were asked if we would be interested in giving a lady and her daughter Bible studies. Of course, we felt unworthy and definitely unequipped, but we agreed. Although reluctant, we felt it would be a great experience while also giving us the possibility to make new friends. Even though it was a good experience, I can't say that we made friends.

It wasn't that we were still new in our beliefs, nor was it the fact that we were mean or anything, but things simply did not work out. In fact, the study lasted for only about five minutes. In hindsight I believe that the reason things didn't work out quite as we had hoped was because it seemed that just maybe the lady might have had an agenda to convert us to her way of thinking. This may sound strange, but right from the start, after nicely getting seated and getting acquainted, the lady asked us a question and was not comfortable with our answer. The question was if we believed in the secret rapture. Even though we had not studied this topic in depth I knew enough about it to answer that we believed in a rapture but not a secret one. But I could not give any particular scriptures to support my answer. The Bible study ended.

The woman told us that if we did not believe in the secret rapture then she had no interest in continuing to study with us. It seems that she had already been told by someone that there would be a secret rapture of the church and therefore the church would not have to go through the time known as the great tribulation. Because this was a comforting thought to her, this lady, who seemed to be very sincere, told us that she was not interested in studying with anyone who didn't believe the same way.

Obviously, we were a little disillusioned with the whole thing as we said our goodbyes and walked to our car. I couldn't help but to think that maybe this Bible study stuff wasn't for us. Nor could I help but to feel a little upset that this woman had wasted our time. But had she?

Maybe it was out of anger, maybe it was pride, maybe a little of both, but for whatever reason, I became determined to learn more about this secret rapture thing. Was it true? If so, where in the Bible could it be found? The next few weeks I found whatever information I could on the subject and learned some surprising things that lead me to believe that God had given us this experience to help us see the big picture even more clearly.

Some may think we are taking a left turn here, however, I have chosen to share this experience because I believe a misunderstanding of this theory can greatly distort one's opinion of God's true character as well. Honestly, as I got into this subject, it caused me quite a lot of disgust almost as much as eternal torment did. Why? Because in this "theory" we can see an apparent insinuation that God and the devil are working together. And, if believed, this theory again intimates an apparent union is designed either to toy with people, or to scare the daylights out of them in hopes that they will repent and come to God.

For those of you are not familiar with the rapture theory let me just say that it is hard to find all the pieces to make any sense out of it whatsoever. In fact, the word rapture cannot be found in the Bible. Yes, there are scriptures that speak of Jesus coming like "a thief in the night" or "one being taken and another left" but as far as any specifics regarding when this will occur, there aren't any. Still, the idea that this is clearly pointed out in the Bible has been accepted by many even today. Why? People want to believe it because it's comforting. But is it true?

If God is going to rapture the church just prior to a seven year tribulation period, doesn't that mean there will be people left behind? The answer is yes. So, do we realize what that means? Just like the idea that the devil is somehow in charge of hell, it means that God and the devil are partners. How can this be? Simply put, if God left people on earth during the tribulation to be manipulated by the antichrist as many believe, He would essentially be allowing the devil to have his way with those left behind.

Whether there would be a second chance for some or not, the idea that God would allow such a thing as some sort of rub-it-in-your-face pre-punishment or scare tactic, this sounds more like a Hollywood movie than something a loving Father would do. And, for those who believe that the church will be raptured in some secret event, I would have to point to many scriptures that describe how noisy the second coming will be. Besides this, there is really no reason for the Bible to mention the second coming of Christ hundreds of times if the saints are already with Him in heaven. Maybe you can tell why I had difficulty believing any of this.

Throughout the Bible there are many examples that show how God prepared His people to go through tribulation. Noah, Joseph, Daniel, and Jesus himself are examples of this fact. These people were prepared to go through trials by putting their faith in the Father who would give them the strength they needed. We can even look to more recent times when millions were tortured through the period known as the Dark Ages as proof that God does not rapture people out of times of tribulation. Are the Christians of today better than those who have previously given their lives for their faith? I think not. As much as the rapture is a nice thing to believe, the theory itself simply does not fit within the scope of sound biblical and historical evidence.

Here's another reason why I could not accept the concept of a secret rapture. And by the way, this was long before the latest book series craze based on this theory. I learned that back in the fifteen hundreds, as part of a counter-reformation tactic, a plan was invented to take the heat off the "church" that was being marked as the antichrist religious system of Bible prophecy. In fact, some pretty scholarly theologians, including Martin Luther, were among those who were said to have fingered the church because of its anti-Bible practices. Therefore, something had to be done. And something was done. That something came in the form of a new interpretation of last day events which would "hopefully" take the heat off the church. Apparently, it has worked.

This new interpretation was loosely based upon a little understood passage in the book of Daniel, chapter nine. This new revelation was used to somehow show that the antichrist could not possibly be the "church" because the true antichrist would not come on the world stage until after the rapture of God's people. In this new theory, the rapture of the church was to occur just prior to a seven-year period known as the great tribulation. When was this seven year period supposed to occur? The rapture is to occur at the beginning of the seventieth week of a 70-week prophecy. However, this dispensationalist theory used some fuzzy math in separating the first sixty-nine weeks of the prophecy from the final, seventieth week by placing two thousand years between them. Can they really do that? Let's read some of the passage in question and see for ourselves. The angle Gabriel is speaking to Daniel.

> Daniel 9:23,24 *At the beginning of thy supplications the commandment came forth, and I am come to shew thee; for thou art greatly beloved: therefore understand the matter, and consider the vision. Seventy weeks are determined upon thy people and upon thy holy city, to finish the transgression, and to make and end of sins, and to make reconciliation for iniquity, and to bring in everlasting righteousness, and to seal up the vision and prophecy, and to anoint the most Holy.*

Basically, in answering a prayer, the angel came to Daniel and was relating to him some conditions from God that must be met during the seventy week time period, in other words, 490 years of prophetic time, (a day for a year, Numbers 14:34). These conditions included anointing Jesus. Let's read on.

> Daniel 9:25,26 *Know therefore and understand, that from the going forth of the commandment to restore and rebuild Jerusalem unto Messiah the Prince shall be seven weeks, and threescore and two weeks: the street shall be built again, and the wall, even in troublous times. And after threescore and two weeks shall Messiah be cut off, but not for himself:*

> Verse 27, *And he shall confirm the covenant with many for one week; and in the midst if the week he shall cause the sacrifice and the oblation to cease...*

According to the prophecy given by the angel, the Messiah would come within a seventy week period, or 490 years. More specifically, the period had a starting point that began with a decree to restore and rebuild Jerusalem 457 BC, and Jesus would arrive on the scene after a seven week, and then a sixty two week period. This sixty-nine weeks or 483 years brings the time to 27 AD, or, the beginning of the seventieth week. Then, Jesus would be cut off. The passage even tells us that whoever this He was, He was not cut off for Himself. That's because this is Jesus who would die for you and me! You see, Jesus was crucified in the middle of the seventieth week and His disciples continued preaching to the Jews for the next three and one half years.

It is amazing how anyone could believe that this is anyone else besides Jesus being described by the angel. But many today think that this is the antichrist and not Christ. And somehow, the world has taken the bait that the seventieth week is yet to be fulfilled. Yes, some believe that there is a 2000 year gap that God had placed between the sixty-ninth and seventieth weeks. By putting this gap in place, many have been misled into thinking that the arrival of the antichrist is way off in the distant future. No, I am not going to tell you who I believe the antichrist is. But study this out and you just might get a pretty good picture of who the devil uses to deceive the world!

Actually, there are many serious problems with this gap theory in addition to the use of fuzzy math. And if you study this entire issue you will see just how silly all of this is. We do not have the time or the space to get into the all of the details in this book, but here are just a few more of the unbiblical components of this weak theory. I give them to you but appeal to you to study this out for yourself.

Secret rapture proponents use as one of there supporting elements the strange idea that the prophets could not see the church age, this 2000 years between the sixty-ninth and seventieth weeks of Daniel's prophecy. This simply does not make any biblical sense whatsoever. Besides, if something like this were true, then it would be the only place in the entire Bible that God would have done such a thing.

Secondly, as I mentioned above, the antichrist that they say was cut-off in the midst of the week is actually Jesus himself as he died three and one half years after his ministry began, causing any meaningful sacrifices to cease. Furthermore, exactly three and one half years later, Stephen, one of the Disciples of Christ, was stoned, marking the end of the seventieth week. Clearly, the stoning of Stephen as recorded in the book of Acts was the end of the seventieth week of Daniel's prophecy.

Yes, the stoning of Stephen essentially ended the Jew's probation period as revealed to Daniel by the angel Gabriel. It sounds like this was bad news for the Jews, and it was. But it was good news for the Gentiles. You see, because the Jews had not accepted Jesus as the Messiah and repented of their sins as Gabriel instructed, they would no longer be used exclusively by God to take the gospel to world. Instead, from the stoning of Stephen onward, the gospel was taken to the Gentiles and salvation would then come to those who would accept Jesus on an individual, and not a national basis.

Can you see how sneaky and potentially harmful all of this is? Could it be possible that the Jews have not accepted the fact that they are no longer God's exclusive messengers to the world? Could it be that their probation period expired because they did not adhere to the conditions laid forth by the angel as presented to Daniel? Is it possible that the Jewish leaders proved their unchanged condition when they stoned Stephen? Could it be that this is why many of them are still refusing to accept Jesus Christ as the Messiah even to this day? Do they really think the seventieth week has not yet been fulfilled? I realize that asking these kinds of questions might make some people uncomfortable but someone has to say something! Whether we want to admit it or not, all of this directly relates to what we understand about God's character and the devil's deceptions.

Getting back to the idea that the seventieth week was not fulfilled, a closer look proves the following. It is Jesus Christ who is the focus of the passage and not the antichrist! Do you remember the account of what happened when Jesus died? How the curtain of the temple was torn? This symbolized the end of the sacrificial system. Yes, He caused the sacrifice and oblation to cease as the passage says. Excuse me for saying this but you Bible scholars just might want to take another look at this issue. Believing that the antichrist is the object of focus in the midst of the week is one of the most terrible distortions of the Bible ever attempted and I believe the devil is behind this deception as well. By taking Jesus out of this passage alters the only text that proves the Messiah came on the scene at the correct prophetic time, and died on time.

Please, please, read the entire chapter of Daniel nine in context. Hopefully, you will see that the seventy weeks is part of the largest time prophecy in the entire Bible, namely, the 2300 day prophecy. And when you re-read the chapter, I believe you will truly be blessed by the type of person Daniel was. He was a very honest and devoted man of God. This is easy to see because the visit from the angel Gabriel was in direct response to one of the most sincere and selfless prayers in the entire Bible. Knowing this will help you to see that God would simply not jerk him around.

And here is another thought. As you know by now I have always attempted to look at things logically assuming that God is logical. Therefore, I did the same thing here. Consider the fact that many movies and books have been written about the rapture, presenting the idea that after this supposed rapture, the Jews and any others that are left behind will be completely ignorant about what is happening. Well, isn't that what is assumed? I say this because apparently the Jews are supposed to get fooled into signing some mock peace accord with a false messiah. Are you with me? Then also consider that after this false messiah allows things to go along smoothly for three and a half years or so, he then is revealed as the antichrist and all hell breaks loose. But here is the big question: How dumb do we think the devil is? I mean, do we really believe that the devil doesn't know that this information is everywhere? Just a little logic here tells me that the deception just might be in this theory and not in what the devil will do to sleepwalking people after the church is in heaven! Am I making any sense here? I'm sorry folks but I simply have to give my Jewish friends a little more credit than that.

Why do I bring all this rapture stuff into the mix? Because it is important to see that there's something seriously wrong with this picture. The whole idea of a secret rapture is simply not in the Bible. And the really sad thing about all this is the fact that this theory itself has really screwed things up in the realms of the religious world. God does not operate in a way that would keep sincere people guessing where He might have moved a very important week. The Bible even tells us that the whole purpose of prophecy is to tell people in advance what will come to pass in the future. And I believe this is especially true if an angel was sent directly to reveal the message. Obviously, God wasn't fooling around in response to Daniel's prayer.

Just think about it: If God were to allow a majority of the people to remain behind after a secret rapture, only to have the devil toy with them, what does that say about God's character? How about you? Would you be happy in heaven knowing that some of your loved ones were going through hell on earth? Remember, the devil will use any and all means, even a secret rapture theory, to counterfeit God's plan and distort our view of the Father's true character. This is serious business!

There is something else about the rapture theory that bothered me when I studied it. The theory itself goes against what the Bible says about <u>when</u> the righteous living will receive their reward.

> 1 Thessalonians 4:16,17 *For the Lord himself shall descend from heaven with a <u>shout</u>, with the voice of the archangel, and with the <u>trump</u> of God: and the <u>dead in Christ shall rise first</u>: Then we which are alive and remain shall be caught up together <u>with them</u> in the clouds, to meet the Lord in the air:*

This is pretty clear... The *dead* in Christ shall rise *first*. Yes, those that are asleep in Jesus will be raised before the living are to be caught up! And here's another very plain passage that shows the second coming of Jesus will not be a secret.

> 2 Peter 3:10 *But the day of the Lord will come as a thief in the night; (unexpected), in the which the heavens shall pass away with a <u>great noise</u>, and the elements shall melt with fervent heat, the earth also and the works that are therein shall be burned up.*

Dear Friends, Jesus is not coming secretly to take the church to heaven prior to a seven-year tribulation period. It may be a nice thing to believe because being raptured before a tribulation period means we wouldn't have to face scary times. But God's word simply does not teach such a thing. It does teach, however, that all believers will put on immortality at the glorious and triumphant second coming of Jesus!

Chapter 19

Wouldn't A God of Love Save Everyone?

Most people would agree that death has caused many tears and grief in the world. No matter who dies, whether grandparents, parents, siblings, babies, other relatives, or friends, death is hard to take. It raises so many questions as to who is really in charge. Natural deaths are easier to accept if someone has lived a long life. But how about the deaths of young children or someone who dies in a freak accident, or because of some terminal disease? Whose fault is that? Is it God's? Maybe I have not mentioned this before so I will say it now... I am very truly sorry for anyone, anywhere who has lost a loved one. It hurts, bad. In fact I cannot even imagine anything worse. So again, please know that I am sorry for your loss.

People wonder how God can allow someone who is loved so much to be taken. I read a really sad classified ad one day where a grieving mother wrote a beautiful tribute to her young daughter. On the anniversary of her daughter's death this mother was struggling to justify her loss by reasoning that God must have loved her little angel more than she did.

How sad. It's sad because of what she went through but even sadder that she was completely unaware that God was weeping with her. God did not take her baby away in some selfish display of control in total disregard for her feelings. No, her baby died because sin and death has contaminated the world.

Where is this dear mother's baby now? Her little angel is asleep in her grave until the resurrection when Jesus returns. Her baby is not in heaven now looking down to see her mommy weeping. Nor is she in purgatory or hell. She is asleep until that great day when this little angel will be reunited with mom. You see, our Heavenly Father is much wiser than we give him credit for.

Some people may have trouble believing that God is Love because of what they have heard or read. Even in the Bible, God can be misunderstood. Yes, throughout history there have been times when God has either allowed humans to be killed, or been actively involved in the destruction of the wicked Himself. But when you really know the whole story you can see that in every event, the death of the rebellious was executed swiftly. No long, drawn out torture, but quick and sudden judgment.

Many times in the history of the world, man has done some pretty awful things. God loves this world but there have been times when He has even regretted creating man because of the evil deeds that have been done to creatures He loves. God knows our hearts. And when we have hardened our hearts beyond the point of no return, He knows we will never be happy continuing down that road. When we are no longer open to the leading of the Holy Spirit and continue in our selfish and destructive ways, the best thing for us is death. Face it, we wouldn't be happy in heaven either.

If you were God, and your children had gone astray, and you could foresee their ultimate doom, what would you do? I truly believe that when God allows wicked people to die, it is an act of mercy. The flood, Sodom and Gomorrah, and Lot's wife are just a few examples of people who did not listen to the warnings from God about their immorality and selfishness. Do you think it is possible that their hearts were hardened beyond hope? It's not only possible, but probable. Remember, the Bible does not contradict itself. Either God is a God of love, or He isn't.

During my studies I was given a book to read which had quite an impact on how I viewed the God of heaven. In this book the writer painted a picture of God being like a loving father. Just like any parent there are times when you have to make some hard decisions. You of course set rules for your children to protect them and must discipline your children if they stray. Sometimes you just have to allow them to make their own mistakes while hoping they don't get hurt through those experiences.

The writer in the book used a very interesting scenario to show how God might think. Assume for a moment that you were the parent of an eight year old boy who had developed a swiftly spreading cancer in his leg. When you speak to the doctor he advises you that you have one of two choices to make. Either you can allow the cancer to spread and take your chances with various therapies that "might" help, or, you could make the choice to amputate the leg and be assured that the child's life will be saved. As difficult a decision that it would be, most parents would probably choose to take the leg. Wouldn't you agree?

When God made this world He said it was good. In His mercy He has allowed man to choose his own way in hopes that eventually we would see the error of our ways and see sin for what it really is. Unfortunately, some have become so hardened with sin and selfishness that they are basically no worldly good, either to themselves or, to the their fellow man. So the question here is, if you were God what would you do?

The Bible says that God so loved the world that He gave his only begotten Son, that man might not perish but have everlasting life. John 3:16. The Bible also tells us that God takes no pleasure in the destruction of the wicked.

> *Ezekiel 33:11 Say unto them, As I live, saith the Lord God, I have no pleasure in the death of the wicked: but that the wicked turn from his way and live: turn ye, turn from your evil ways: for why will ye die, Oh house of Israel?*

Does this sound like a God who is mixed up? I don't think so. The God I have come to know is very loving, merciful, and logical. And He has developed a tremendous plan for overcoming the problem of sin and death for each and every one of us. Our heavenly Father is not only a God of Love, but also a God of justice. And although He is merciful and longsuffering He will not tolerate the degradation of this world forever. There will come a time that each and every person will have made their decision. They will either choose sin and selfishness, basically honoring the devil, or they will clearly see the terrible tragedies that sin has caused and choose God's way.

Very soon the two sides will be determined and there will be two rewards, one for each side. These two sides are the wicked (dead and living), and the righteous (dead and living). No ghosts, no purgatory, no raptured saints coming back to claim their decomposed bodies. Simply and clearly the Bible tells us that all those who are in their graves are awaiting their reward.

> *Revelation 22:11 He that is unjust, let him be unjust still: and he that is filthy, let him be filthy still: and he that is righteous, let him be righteous still: and he that is holy, let him be holy still. And behold, I come*

> quickly; and my reward is with me, to give <u>every</u> man according as his work shall be.

Yes, there are only two groups and Jesus is coming back to reward both of them.

> John 5:29 *Marvel not at this: for the hour is coming, in the which <u>all</u> that are in the graves shall hear his voice, And shall come forth; they that have done good, unto the resurrection of life; and they that have done evil, unto the resurrection of damnation.*

As I have said many times the Bible is clear on this subject. People simply do not receive their reward, whether good or bad, until the second coming of Jesus. He is the only one who can give the reward of eternal life because He is the only one who has defeated death. Humans are just not immortal no matter how you slice it. As hard as this is for some, you simply cannot get around God's word. When you really think about it, Jesus would not have had to die a cruel death to save people from the wages of their sins if everyone is immortal anyway, right?

Never would I have imagined that my heartache over the fate of my loved ones would have led me to this point. I really had no idea all that was at stake. From the very beginning of the creation of the world it seems that the issue of death has been at the forefront of virtually everything. God created us and wants us to be with him for eternity. However, He just can't allow sin to rise up a second time.

> Nahum 1:7-9 *The Lord is good, a strong hold in the day of trouble; and he knoweth them that trust him. But with an overwhelming flood he will make an utter end of the place thereof, and darkness shall pursue his enemies. What do ye imagine against the Lord?*

He will make an utter end: affliction shall not rise up the second time.

God does not want sin and rebellion to continue. For that reason the wicked will ultimately be destroyed. But it is clear that their destruction will not be in an eternally burning hell. God's mercy is such that He will not torture those who deny His way. He will simply and swiftly perform what the Bible calls His strange act. But this strange act is not that strange when you really understand its purpose. Yes, it may sound strange that this loving Father as described in this book would put an end to sin by destroying the devil and all the wicked. And that's just the point. It's strange for Him because it goes against His character. However, maybe it is not a strange act at all when we understand that it is harbored sin within man himself in the presence of a Holy God that destroys the wicked.

Romans 2:5 *But after thy hardness and impenitent heart treasurest up unto thyself wrath against the day of wrath and revelation of the righteous judgment of God;*

Hebrews 12:28,29 *Wherefore we receiving a kingdom which cannot be moved, let us have grace, whereby we may serve God acceptably with reverence and godly fear: For our God is a consuming fire.*

Yes, man will be destroyed because he has chosen to embrace sin over the goodness of God. In fact, wicked man cannot survive in the presences of a holy God. We must understand that our Father takes no pleasure in that choice but it is ours to make. He warns us repeatedly about turning from sin because He does not want us to be destroyed. This confirms again that what I believed in the beginning; that death is a bad thing. It seems God thinks so too. This is why death will ultimately be destroyed in the lake of fire, proving once again that there can not possibly be a place of eternal torment.

1 Corinthians 15:26 *The last enemy that shall be destroyed is death.*

Revelation 20:14 *And death and hell were cast into the lake of fire.*

It has been a long time since I have brought up my brother, but during this process I thought about him an awful lot. I do not know for sure what side he will be on when all is said and done. However, among other things, I am certain that God didn't take Bobby from us. No, my brother died because this world is full of sin, sickness, and death. In addition, learning that my brother may have been over exposed to radiation, along with knowing he did not always make the best health choices, really takes the mystery away. God did not take him because He had some job for him to do. No, my brother is currently sleeping the sleep of death, completely unaware of anything going on in the world.

I do not know what Bobby was thinking toward the end of his life or if he asked for his sins to be forgiven. Honestly, I am not even sure he knew what sin was or if he really understood the issues relating to this cosmic battle. But knowing that God is merciful and compassionate, I believe He gave my brother every opportunity to know good from evil and make his decision.

When Bobby died of cancer the only good thing I could see was that he was no longer suffering. And all those other questions added grief because I simply did not have a clue as to what the possibilities were. But now, as I have learned what happens at death, I do not fear that he is burning forever, nor do I think about him watching me and the rest of the family toiling through this life on earth.

Do I know for sure what will be my Brother's fate? Only God knows. He was a good kid with a big heart but I just don't know for sure what will happen on the last day. Of course, my hope is that he will be raised in the first resurrection, the resurrection of the righteous. In fact, my hope is for all my loved ones and friends to be resurrected with the righteous and be in heaven. However, I am no longer naive about this subject. As much as we want to believe that all people will be in paradise, the chances of that are pretty slim. Why do I say that? Jesus said it.

> Matthew 7:13,14 *Enter ye in at he strait gate: for wide is the gate, and broad is the way, that leadeth to destruction, and many there be which go in thereat: Because strait is the gate, and narrow is the way, which leadeth unto life, and few there be that find it.*

I have come to realize that it is not enough to simply know the truth but we must act upon what we know. The Bible even says that "faith without works is dead." James 2:20. And even Jesus himself made the same point when he said, "Be doers of the word and not hearers only." James 1:22. I am afraid that most people in the world are just hearers. They mean well but never really take their faith to the level of giving up the things that separate them from God. I know this because it was that way for me for a long time. But because everything was all coming together in seemingly perfect logic, it was about time that I considered taking my faith to the next level.

Chapter 20

Is God Really Like a Loving Father?

From everything I had learned, probably the most important thing was that of realizing just how true the Bible was in describing God as Love. And, quite simply, I really had no desire to be in heaven if it were any different. I'm just too much of a simpleton to struggle with this. I had determined on this journey to either choose to follow, or not. Remaining on the fence was just not an option for me. Somehow believing God as being one who gave His Son to take our punishment did not fit with the character of someone who is planning to burn sinners forever. Honestly, for the first time in my life I was beginning to know, and actually sympathize with God.

> 1 John 4:9 *He that loveth not knoweth not God; for God is love.*

> Matthew 1:21 *And she shall bring forth a son, and thou shalt call his name JESUS: for he shall save his people from their sins.*

What a gift! Up until this point I did not realize what amazing grace really was. But in this last text from Matthew I noticed an important point that should be brought out here. Notice the text doesn't say that he will save people *in* their sins, but *from* their sins. Not only does this mean we can be saved from the penalty of our sins, or death, but through the power of the Holy Spirit we can also forsake sin and use our appreciation as motivation to honor God and serve sin no more. You see, sin is why Jesus had to go through death to begin with. Because of scriptures like this I began to picture God as the best Father and provider anyone could ever have. But it was not always this way. Yes, I once thought of God as some mysterious and distant force who was not interested in the lives of little people like me. But as my eyes were opened to many of the facts presented in this book, my view had completely changed.

I was now realizing that the Father that I had not known for most of my life loved me so much. He had provided a wonderful place for me to live with everything I could possibly need. In this world filled with so much beauty and balance I could see wonderful mountains, beautiful sunrises over the ocean, gorgeous plants and animals and awesome night skies. My father had given me air to breathe, water to drink, as well as food, shelter and clothing, and allowed me to truly experience this entire creation with no restrictions. This doesn't sound like a bad father so far, does it?

Just like any good parent would establish rules to protect their children, my Father has done that too. He didn't want me to burn my hand on the stove, get hit by a car or harm someone else, so he has taught me what is right and wrong and told me about the possible consequences of my disobedience. He has done this because he loves me. My father is sad when I hurt, and He is happy when I am happy. He has told me that he will never leave me or forsake me which helps me always feel wanted. And when it is time for me to go to sleep, He is there to make sure I am safely tucked in my bed. My father makes sure I am not afraid, and he even kisses me on the forehead while he hugs me and says goodnight. If this is not enough, my father tells me he loves me while looking back once again before the light goes out. Then, he tells me that he will see me in the morning. And you know what? This is exactly what happens when people die when they have a relationship with Him!

It is so sad to see and hear of people who don't know God in this way. Because they have lost a parent, a sibling, a child or close friend, many feel that God is not as loving as they would like to believe. Some wonder how God could possibly allow so much pain and suffering to continue. How is it that there are so many people starving? Why so many natural disasters? While writing this book my brother-in-law's wife died of cancer leaving behind a husband and three children. How could God allow that? One reason these things happen is because sin has contaminated our world. Because of the devil's deceptions in the garden and wrong choices of our first parents, this world has been on a downward spiral.

Could God have stopped this degradation of mankind? Sure He could have. But because of His love, He has allowed man to make his own choices. From the beginning He has been accused by the devil of wanting to control all of His creatures, but this is simply not God's nature. Because of His love for us, He will allow us to exercise our own free will, all the while hoping that we eventually will see the error of our ways and come home. In the mean time, life and death continue.

As the devil deceives more people into believing his lies about God's character, the more the world is tarnished. All we need to do is look around at the world today to know this is true. Have we really been so good enough as to think that nothing bad will happen? Most of us would have to admit that we have done something to hurt ourselves, someone else, the earth, or even God Himself. And when we think about how things will be in heaven if sin is allowed to continue, we can see why God will sooner or later have to stop the madness. But in the meantime, He is patiently waiting.

> 2 Peter 3:9 *The Lord is not slack concerning his promise, as some men count slackness; but is longsuffering to us-ward, not willing that any should perish, but that all should come to repentance.*

We all make mistakes. However, when those mistakes turn into outright rebellion to the point of becoming habitual, then we have two choices. Either we can ask God to help us, or we can continue in our selfish ways. If we choose the latter, how do you think that makes the Father feel? I'm sure He is greatly saddened when we have come to love sin more than Him. This is because He knows what the final result will be. Just like when a parent knows that playing on a busy street could mean tragedy, God also knows that when we flirt with danger, bad things will result. Furthermore, if a person goes beyond the point of hearing the voice of the Holy Spirit, then God knows it will be better for them if they did not continue on that destructive path.

Sin will not be allowed into heaven a second time and the reason for this is quite simple. You see, if sin and rebellion are allowed to continue, then heaven just wouldn't be heaven. Many today are hoping for a day when they can live in peace and harmony with no more pain, tears, sickness and death. I sure am.

In the previous chapters I have mentioned the death of many loved ones in my own family. From my brother to the recent death of a sister-in-law, all were very sad events. Death is just something that every family will have to face. In fact, death continues to be the most dominating source of pain in my life today. Just how dominating? In the short period of time that this book was being written our family has not only lost a sister-in-law, but I learned of the death of a childhood friend to cancer, my own Godfather who died after a long illness, a coworker's niece who died of cancer at the tender age of seventeen, and an elderly brother from a local church, again from cancer. There have also been many deaths as reported in the media as I have continued to write. Of course we all know about the death of Pope John Paul II and all of the coverage relating to his sickness and death. And, who can forget Terri Schiavo? She was the woman who died after being taken off life support. Death is everywhere and will continue to be everywhere until Jesus returns and puts an end to sickness and death. Yes, Jesus will return. And when He does He will reward every person, either with eternal life in heaven, or their lives will perish swiftly and mercifully.

With all the clear evidence the Bible gives, I do not even consider the thought that any of the above mentioned people are now in heaven. This may sound harsh in light of the fact that some were very close to me. But, I know now there is simply no scriptural or logical evidence that supports the idea that the bodies or souls of these mortals are currently anywhere but in the grave. The same goes for the pope and even the Virgin Mary as well. No matter how great these people might have been, it is only the spirit, or breath of life, that returns to God upon death. The soul is simply not immortal.

Looking back, it seems that the only real scary thing about death was the unknown. I guess if you have knowledge of the truth but know you are unrepentant and unprepared to die, I guess that could be a little scary as well. But for a Christian who has the understanding of what really happens at death, there is really nothing to fear at all. You see, of all the people mentioned above who have recently died, only two that I know of faced death knowing the things that you have learned in this book. It was the young seventeen year old and the elder from the local church.

Even though these two had suffered greatly with the pain of a terrible disease, they put their faith and trust in the Father because they were secure in their understanding that they would be resurrected on the last day! They knew that they would be raised together to meet Jesus face to face when He returns after preparing a place for them. They knew that God not only loved them but He has also made provision for them. And just as it were no more than a twinkling of an eye, the next thing they will know is to see Jesus coming in great power and glory to take them home. And one more very important point... they also knew they would not be in heaven looking down upon those they left behind, and watching them weeping and struggling to make it through their days.

When you really stop and think about it, belief in a Creator God who made and cares for us all, is really a very liberating idea. That is, if you know Him. It's hard to see where any other belief system in our world today can even begin to compare with one in which a personal God is pulling for you all the way. Many of the world's religious systems of the day are greatly dependant upon man obtaining their own merits or because of some rituals they perform that somehow deem them holy. But let's face it, none us are good enough based on our own merits, nor can we earn our way into immortality. Again, in these strange forms of religion we see the devil's lie. But Christianity, on the other hand, is the only system where the hope of man is based solely upon the merits of God. Did you get that? Christianity is the only religion based solely, and grounded upon the goodness of God and His grace. This is huge friend, especially in light of the fact that God loves us so much!

When I learned that God wanted to be with us for eternity so much that He came to earth in the person of His Son

Questioning Death

to pay our debt and die in our place, I knew this was real. What other religion can stake its faith upon a God who is not only a loving Creator, but who is also our Redeemer, Attorney, Advocate and Judge? That's right, none.

If you want to find your own way to heaven, go for it. Do you think you have what it takes to obtain immortality on your own? Good luck. Do you have faith in yourself because you perform some ritual or because you have kissed the feet of some statue? Be my guest. Maybe you choose to chant repetitious prayers which fall upon the deaf ears of some exalted but long-since dead saint. If this is your hope, my prayer is that you will pray to the living Savior instead.

Proverbs 14:12 *There is a way which seemeth right unto a man, but the end thereof are the ways of death.*

I am sorry if it sounds like I am condemning the religious practices of sincere people. Many just do not know better because they have followed in the traditions of their fathers and forefathers. But dear friends, this stuff is not as complicated as many men, or the devil, would have you to believe. In fact, it's as simple as black and white, even the black and white pages of this simple little book and many others like it. But sometimes it's hard to pull away from traditional thinking and see the truth that God wants us to see.

It matters not where you are now in your spiritual walk. And it doesn't even matter where you've been. What matters is where you are going from this point on. Do you really know the Father? If not, you can start all over today. Simply throw away all of those confusing, preconceived ideas and lies of the devil that insinuate that we are immortal, or, that we can somehow find our own way to eternal life. Quite frankly, you are not immortal, nor are any of us good enough to make it to heaven on our own. Boy, its sure is nice to know that Jesus is good enough!

> John 14:2,3 *In my Father's house are many mansions: if it were not so, I would have told you. And if I go and prepare a place for you, I will come again, and receive you unto myself; that where I am, there ye may be also.*

Chapter 21

Will Simply Believing In Jesus Get Me Into Heaven?

I have mixed feeling when I share what I learned about the fact that there will be those that will be very happy when Jesus comes back, but others won't be. Some will receive the gift of eternal life (immortality) because they have put their full trust in Him. But sadly, some won't. The later group won't be given life, but death. This is because they had simply rejected the gift offered by Jesus and chose to do things their own way. Jesus told us that even among the ranks of those who call themselves His followers, many will be lost…

> Matthew 7:21-23 *Not every one that saith unto me, Lord, Lord, shall enter into the kingdom of heaven; but he that doeth the will of my Father which is in heaven. Many will say to me in that day, Lord, Lord, have we not prophesied in thy name? And in thy name have cast out devils? And in thy name done many wonderful works? And then I will profess unto*

them, I never knew you: depart from me, ye that work iniquity.

For over thirty years I heard mostly confusion and contradictions from the pulpit. Sure, I did very little on my own to learn the truth but just maybe the mixed messages about God's character had something to do with that. I'll even go so far as to say that the contradictions among the Christian leaders of this era have most likely contributed to my parents and grandparents being somewhat disillusioned as well. Yes, the devil has to take a majority of the blame here but it pains me even today to think about how supposed men of the cloth could actually be doing the church more damage than good. It's sad to think that even among the ranks of Christianity many will be deemed unworthy. Could it be this is because they have believed in a God who would burn people for eternity? From what I know now, I believe it is.

God wants all people to clearly know the issues relating to His character and His love for mankind. He wants us to know that sin and death separate us from Him and will keep us from enjoying eternal life in heaven. We simply cannot remain on the fence. Satan owns the fence! I believe God also wants the world to know that you don't have to be a theologian, minister or priest to know the truth as written in the Bible. Each and every person can and should be able to learn about Jesus and the great sacrifice He made for you and me. He made this sacrifice because He knows that death is bad.

2 Timothy 1:10 *But is now made manifest by the appearing of our Savior Jesus Christ, who hath abolished death, and hath brought life and immortality to light through the gospel.*

For those who accept the sacrifice of God's son for forgiveness of their sins, when they die, their death is like an unconscious sleep until the resurrection when Jesus returns. But for those who do not accept this sacrifice, they will not obtain eternal life; neither in heaven, nor in some eternal pit called hell. No, eternal life will not be given to everybody. Unfortunately, the Bible teaches that many who think they will be given immortality and a place in heaven will be greatly disappointed.

Is it possible that even among the ranks of church goers some will not make it? That's what the Bible teaches. But just what is it that might keep a person from knowing the truth and having the assurance that they will be on the right side in the end? In a word, lies. Yes, I believe that lies about souls burning eternally caused people like Robert Ingersol and Charles Darwin to deny the idea of a loving Father. As a result these very bright men sought to uncover other possible reasons for man's existence.

It is also possible that those who had witnessed, or even learned of, the terrible crimes committed in the name of God during the Dark Ages believe God is a mean God. It is truly sad to learn that those who committed those awful crimes against humanity were not working for God at all. The only thing that would be even remotely defensible would be if they really believed they were ushering their victims into eternal life. But here again, we have a lie. If there is any doubt about who was behind these cruel murders, consider the fact that many of the martyrs were tortured before being put to death. This is proof as to who these people were working for. Can you see how this all works to deceive the world and distort the character of God? And much of this was done in the name of religion. The more I dug, the more sickening all of this became.

Must we even question why people are reluctant to know God better? Let's face it folks, the church today is a mess. With sex and money scandals, debates over gay bishops, gay marriages, arguments over the place of the Ten Commandments in the church, belief in the immortality of the soul, prayers for the dead, secret raptures, etc., it's no wonder why people are so disillusioned. How many religious groups do we have in the world today, thousands? And isn't it true that there are at least hundreds of Christian denominations? Do we think that this might be just a little confusing? I hate to say it but my Bible states very clearly that there is one Lord, one Faith and one baptism. Ephesians 4:5. You sure wouldn't know it by looking at the religious world today.

I used to look up to the Christian church in general as a shinning beacon of light in a dark world. This was when I had no clue about anything religious whatsoever. I also thought that anyone who was really a Christian basically had their ticket to heaven when they died. But as I learned more and more about this issue of death and the great battle regarding truth, the more I began to believe that even in the ranks of Christianity many people will be lost. This is not because they are not sincere, but because they simply do not know the God who they claim to worship. It seems to me that many people simply go through the motions and follow along in hopes of being on the right track. Am I wrong in this assumption?

In the book of Revelation we find a very clear picture of the two distinct groups in question. No, it's not Christians and Muslims, Jews and everybody else, nor is it believers in a god as apposed to those who are unbelievers. Quite simply, the Bible teaches that these two groups are those who know and love the Creator, and those who might have a form of faith but continue in iniquity by following the devil's counterfeits. Of course, the counterfeits include just about everything else. You know... the worship of nature, or some planetary gods, the love of money and material things, the worship of men as if they are gods themselves, and the list goes on and on.

In fact, we can also throw apostate Christianity into the mix as well. Basically, anything the devil can use to divert your worship from the true Creator is in some twisted way, honor he claims for himself.

There is great importance attached to this issue of worship in the scriptures. In fact, the book of Revelation identifies two distinct groups who show their loyalty to either the true God, or to a mixed up conglomerate of false religions. Another interesting point is that God uses a woman when referring to His church. See Jeremiah 6:2. However, in the book of Revelation, God also uses a woman to describe this false system. Notice the stark difference between these two women.

> Revelation 17:3-6 *So he carried me away in the spirit into the wilderness; and I saw a woman sit upon a scarlet coloured beast, full of names of blasphemy, having seven heads and ten horns. And the woman was arrayed in purple and scarlet colour, and decked with gold and precious stones and pearls, having a golden cup in her hand full of abominations and filthiness of her fornication: And upon her forehead was a name written, MYSTERY, BABYLON THE GREAT, THE MOTHER OF HARLOTS AND ABOMINATIONS OF THE EARTH. And I saw the woman drunken with the saints, and with the blood of the martyrs of Jesus:*

Just think of it... if Satan is the father of lies, and Babylon symbolizes the Mother of Harlots, who is linked with the abominations of the earth, this could very well mean that the mother herself, as well as the many daughters, are all part of a system which perpetuates the devil's lies and confusion. This is not only possible, but from my perspective, it is exactly what we see today. Even though many believe that all roads lead to heaven, and that it really doesn't matter what religious group you belong to, God sees things quite differently. Yes, He definitely makes it clear that there are only two sides.

How about the other woman? What is her character?

This other woman is depicted as a pure woman, the Bride of Christ. As you read this passage please pay special attention to what the devil wants to do to this pure woman.

> *Revelation 12:1-2, 5, 9,13,17 And there appeared a great wonder in heaven; a woman clothed with the sun, and the moon under her feet, and upon her head a crown of twelve stars: And she being with child cried, travailing in birth, and pained to be delivered. (5) And she brought forth a man child, who was to rule all nations with a rod of iron: and her child was caught up unto God, and to his throne. (9) And the great dragon was cast out, that old serpent, called the Devil and Satan, which deceiveth the whole world: (13) And when the dragon saw that he was cast unto the earth, he persecuted the woman which brought fourth the man child. (17) And the dragon was wroth with the woman, and went to make war with the remnant of her seed, which keep the commandments of God, and have the testimony of Jesus Christ.*

Maybe you can now see why the passage we read from Revelation seventeen states that the first woman is drunken with the blood of the saints. This is because Babylon, or this conglomeration of all false religions, is a tool for the devil to attack the true church. Satan not only tried to destroy Jesus from the beginning, but has continued to destroy God's true church ever since. Why? It's because he knows that they have the truth that can unmask his bag of lies. Hopefully, you also notice that this remnant Satan is after is said to keep the commandments of God. This may not sound like a big deal, however, it is. And Satan knows it.

Unfortunately, this little book cannot contain the detailed history of this ongoing controversy. But I hope you can at least see the two sides here. In the end there will be the Bride of Christ, and a conglomerate of all the rest. I encourage each reader to look around the world today and watch these two women as they become more and more distinct from one another. And as you see this happening, get into your Bible. God will show you what you need to know.

So again I ask the same question. What is it that might keep a person from knowing the truth and having the assurance that they will be on the right side in the end? The answer... lies, confusion, and deception, or in other words, the works of Satan. By distorting the truth about the character of God and the immortality of the soul, and by conjuring up all other forms of false religions, Satan has almost succeeded in deceiving the entire world. I use the term almost because he will not succeed. He knows that he will lose in the end and is not the least bit happy about it. In fact, he knows the Bible better than humans do and is fully aware that he is a defeated foe. But while God mercifully waits for all who will seek the truth and come to Him, the devil will continue to deceive in an attempt to turn as many against God as he can.

I hope the devil's lies will not work on you friend. They did on me for a long time but I am so grateful that God pulled me out of the darkness.

Chapter 22

How Does All of This Information Fit Together?

So what happens to a person if they do <u>not</u> go directly to heaven upon death? What will be the reward of the people who accept the blood of Jesus to cover their sins? When will they receive their reward? And how about those who choose to deny God's love and follow the devil? What will be their reward and when will they receive it? The Bible has the answers. Because it is my desire to clearly share what I have learned on this quest for answers, the format of this chapter will be somewhat different.

I am going to take you step by step through a series of many of the same questions recorded in this book but with a big-picture perspective. I want you all to see how everything we have learned can be logically connected and how this issue relates to the judgment when each person receives their reward. Allowing the Bible to answer any remaining questions is the best way I could think to tie this all together. This process not only helped me to fill in any blanks that I had not yet grasped, but also helped me to see the beauty and completeness of God's word.

You will notice that in some cases I have not given the entire answering text. Not only has this been done in order to save time and space, but also to encourage every reader to look up the scripture references for themselves. Like I have stated many times before, please do not take anyone else's word for anything!

What did God use to create man?
Genesis 2:7 *And God formed man from the dust of the earth and breathed into his nostrils the breath of life and man became a living soul.*

Does this mean that a living soul and a living being are the same thing?
Leviticus 5:1 *If a soul touch any unclean thing...*
Leviticus 17:12 *...no soul of you shall eat blood...*
Job 6:7 *The things that my soul refused to touch...*
Act 2:41 *Then they that gladly received his word were baptized: and the same day there were added unto them about three thousand souls.*

So it is the breath of life, or spirit, from God that gives man life?
Genesis 6:17 *And, behold, I, even I, do bring a flood of waters upon the earth, to destroy all flesh, wherein is the breath of life...*
Job 27:3 *All the while my breath is in me, and the spirit of God is in my nostrils...*

What happens to the breath, or spirit, at death?
Psalm 146:4 *His breath goeth forth, he returneth to his earth...*
Eccl 12:7 *Then shall the dust return to the earth as it was: and the spirit shall return unto God who gave it.*

And how about the body. Where does it go?

Job 10:9 *Remember, I beseech thee, that thou hast made me as the clay; and wilt thou bring me to dust again?*
Job 34:15 *...and man shall turn again into dust.*
Psalm 104:29 *Thou hidest thy face, they are troubled: thou takest away their breath, they die, and return to their dust.*

Does this mean a soul can die?

Ezekiel 18:20 *The soul that sinneth, it shall die.*
James 5:20 *Let him know, that he which converteth the sinner from the error of his way, shall save a soul from death...*

Do dead souls know, or do anything?

Psalm 146:4 *His breath goeth forth, he returneth to his earth; in that very day his thoughts perish.*
Ecclesiastes 9:5 *For the living know that they shall die: but the dead know not any thing...*
Ecclesiastes 9:10 *Whatsoever thy hand findeth to do, do it with thy might; for there is no work, nor device, nor knowledge, nor wisdom, in the grave, whither thou goest.*

Does the Bible really refer to death as a sleep?

Job 7:21 *...for now shall I sleep in the dust; and thou shalt seek me in the morning, but I shall not be.*
Job 14:12 *So man lieth down, and riseth not: till the heavens be no more, they shall not awake, nor be raised out of their sleep.*
Psalm 13:3 *Consider and hear me, O Lord my God: lighten my eyes, lest I sleep the sleep of death.*

According to the Bible, who currently has immortality?
1 Tim 1:17 *Now unto the King eternal, immortal, invisible, the only wise God, be honour and glory for ever and ever, Amen.*
1 Tim 6:15,16 *...the blessed and only Potentate, the King of kings, and Lord of lords: Who only hath immortality...*

Does this mean that no humans are currently in heaven?
A Special Note: The possibility exists that Enoch was translated without seeing death. Elijah is said to have been seen riding into the heavens on a chariot. Both of these men had very close walks with God and may have had been given special passage. This means they did not die an earthly death and therefore, would not have go through the process of putting on immortality at the last trump. Moses also had a close walk with God and when he died no man knew where his body was buried. It is believed that Moses may have been resurrected in a special resurrection. On the mount of transfiguration the witnesses reported seeing two figures who appeared to be Moses and Elijah. It is believed that these two beloved men where there to encourage Jesus. Moses would represent those who would be resurrected at the second coming (the righteous dead), while Elijah would represent those who would be living when Christ returns, (the righteous living). However, at the transfiguration, the disciples were told not to tell anyone about the *vision*. Meaning that this was a vision of the future. Other than these special men who may have been given immortality, there is no record of any others being translated. The remaining people, both living and dead, will not receive their reward until the second coming of Christ.

Questioning Death

Since the dead are in their graves, when will they receive their reward, or punishment?

1 Thessalonians 4:13, 16,17 *But I would not have you to be ignorant, brethren, concerning them which are asleep, that ye sorrow not, even as others which have no hope... For the Lord himself shall descend from heaven with a shout, with the voice of the archangel, and the trump of God: and the dead in Christ shall rise first: Then we which are alive and remain shall be caught up together with them in the clouds, to meet the Lord in the air; and so shall we ever be with the Lord.*

Dan 12:2 *And many of them that sleep in the dust of the earth shall awake, some to everlasting life, and some to shame and everlasting contempt.*

Didn't Jesus say He went to prepare a place for the righteous?

John 14:1-3 *Let not your heart be troubled: ye believe in God, believe also in me. In my Father's house are many mansions: if it were not so, I would have told you. I go to prepare a place for you. And if I go and prepare a place for you, I will come again, and receive you unto myself; that where I am, there ye may be also.*

When will Jesus return?

Mat 24:36,37 *But of that day and hour knoweth no man, no, not the angels of heaven, but my Father only. But as the days of Noe were, so shall also the coming of the Son of man be...*

2 Thes 2:1-3 *Now we beseech you, brethren, by the coming of our Lord Jesus Christ, and by our gathering together unto him, That ye be not soon shaken in mind, or be troubled, neither by spirit, nor by word, nor by letter as from us, as that the day of Christ is at hand. Let no man deceive you by any means: for that day shall not*

come, except there come a falling away first, and that man of sin be revealed, the son of perdition...
Revelation 5:2,9 *And I saw a strong angel proclaiming with a loud voice, Who is worthy to open the book, and to loose the seals thereof? And they sung a new song, saying, Thou art worthy to take the book, and to open the seals thereof: for thou wast slain, and hast redeemed us to God by thy blood...*

What is meant by the opening of the book and loosening the seals?

Please read Revelation chapter six. The book is the book of life and the removing of the seals releases the seven last plagues. This is the beginning of God's judgment of the earth.

Does this mean the judgment occurs before the plagues and the coming of Jesus?

Daniel 7:9,10 *I beheld til the thrones were cast down, and the Ancient of days did sit; whose garment was white as snow, and the hair of his head like the pure wool: his throne was like the fiery flame, and his wheels as burning fire. A fiery stream issued and came forth from before him: thousand thousands ministered unto him, and ten thousand times ten thousand stood before him: the judgment was set, and the books were opened.*
Revelation 11: 18,19 *And the nations were angry, and thy wrath is come, and the time of the dead, that they should be judged, and that thou shouldest give reward unto thy servants the prophets, and to the saints, and them that fear thy name, small and great; and shouldest destroy them which destroy the earth.*
Revelation 20:11 *And I saw the dead, small and great, stand before God; and the books were opened: and another book was opened, which is the book of life: and*

the dead were judged out of those things which were written in the books, according to their works.

How will the righteous be able to make it through the seven last plagues and God's wrath while waiting for Jesus to come?

Psalm 91:4-11 *He shall cover thee with his feathers, and under his wings shall thou trust: his truth shall be thy shield and buckler. Thou shall not be afraid for the terror by night; nor for the arrow that flieth by day; Nor for the pestilence that walketh in darkness; nor for the destruction that wasteth at noonday. A thousand shall fall at thy side. And ten thousand at thy right hand; but it shall not come nigh thee. Only with thine eyes shalt thou behold and see the reward of the wicked. Because thou hast made the Lord, which is my refuge, even the most High, thy habitation; There shall be no evil befall thee, neither shall any plague come nigh thy dwelling. For he shall give his angels charge over thee, to keep thee in all thy ways.*

Will the coming of Christ be a secret or quiet event?

1 Thessalonians 4:16,17 *For the Lord himself shall descend from heaven with a <u>shout</u>, with the voice of the archangel, and with the trump of God: and the dead in Christ shall rise first:*
2 Peter 3:10 *But the day of the Lord will come as a thief in the night; in the which the heavens shall pass away with a <u>great noise</u>, and the elements shall melt with fervent heat, the earth also and the works that are therein shall be burned up.*

Can we know when we are getting close to the end of the age and the coming of Christ?

Matthew 24 (Please read the entire chapter)

2 Timothy 3:1-5 *This know also, that in the last days perilous times shall come. For men shall be lovers of their own selves, covetous, boasters, proud, blasphemers, disobedient to parents, unthankful, unholy. Without naturals affection, trucebreakers, false accusers, incontinent, fierce, despisers of those that are good, Traitors, heady, highminded, lovers of pleasure more than lovers of God: Having a form of godliness, but denying the power thereof: from such turn away.*

What is the reward for those who are judged righteous?

Isaiah 25:8,9 *He will swallow up death in victory; and the Lord God will wipe away tears from all faces; and the rebuke of his people shall he take away from off all the earth: for the Lord hath spoken it. And it shall be said in that day, Lo, this is our God; we have waited for him, and he will save us...*

Matthew 5:12 *Rejoice, and be exceeding glad: for great is your reward in heaven...*

2 Timothy 4:8 *Henceforth there is laid up for me a crown of righteousness, which the Lord, the righteous judge, shall give me at that day: and not to me only, but unto all them also that love his appearing.*

Is the reward the same for the righteous, both the dead and the living?

1 Corinthians 15:51 *Behold, I shew you a mystery; We shall not all sleep, but we shall all be changed, In a moment, in the twinkling of an eye, at the last trump: for the trumpet shall sound, and the dead shall be raised incorruptible, and we shall be changed. For this corruption must put on incorruption, and this mortal must put on immortality.*

1 Thessalonians 4:16,17 *...and the dead in Christ shall rise first: Then we which are alive and remain shall be*

caught up together with them in the clouds, to meet the Lord in the air: and so shall we ever be with the Lord.
Revelation 20:4,5,6 ...and they lived and reigned with Christ a thousand years...This is the first resurrection. Blessed and holy is he that hath part in the first resurrection: on such the second death hath no power, but they shall be priests of God and Christ, and shall reign with him a thousand years.

What happens to the wicked who are in their graves when Jesus returns?

Revelation 20:5 *But the rest of the dead lived not again until the thousand years were finished.*
John 5:28,29 *Marvel not at this: for the hour is coming, in the which all that are in the graves shall hear his voice, And shall come forth; they that have done good, unto the resurrection of life; (first resurrection) and they that have done evil, unto the resurrection of damnation. (second resurrection).*

If any of the wicked can survive the seven last plagues, what happens to them when Jesus comes to redeem the righteous?

2 Thessalonians 2:8,10 *And then shall that Wicked be revealed, whom the Lord shall consume with the spirit of his mouth, and shall destroy with the brightness of his coming: And with all deceivableness of unrighteousness in them that perish; because they received not the love of the truth, that they might be saved.*

What happens to the devil at the second coming?

Revelation 20:1-3 *And I saw an angel come down from heaven, having the key of the bottomless pit and a great chain in his hand. And he laid hold on the dragon, that old serpent, which is the Devil, and Satan, and bound* him a thousand years. And cast him into the bottomless pit, and shut him up, and set a seal upon him, that he should deceive the nations no more, till the thousand years should be fulfilled: and after that he must be loosed a little season.

Does anything happen during the thousand years?
1 Corinthians 6:2 *Do ye not know that the saints shall judge the world?*
Revelation 16:5,7 *And I heard the angel of the waters say, Thou art righteous, O Lord, which art, and wast, and shall be, because thou hast judged thus. And I heard another out of the alter say, Even so, Lord God Almighty, true and righteous are thy judgments.*

Note: Basically, God allows the saints to examine the books. This is because God himself has been on trial as Satan has accused Him of being unjust. What the saints learn is that God has been very patient with us and He has given every opportunity for each person to accept His love and salvation. But as all of heaven is witness, the wicked once again show their true colors.

What happens after the thousand years?
Revelation 21: 2 *And I John, saw the holy city, new Jerusalem, coming down from God out of heaven, prepared as a bride adorned for her husband.*
Revelation 20:7-10 *And when the thousand years are expired, Satan shall be loosed out of his prison, And shall go out to deceive the nations which are in the four quarters of the earth, Gog and Magog, to gather them to battle: the number of whom is as the sand of the sea. And they went up on the breadth of the earth, and compassed the camp of the saints about, and the beloved city...*

Who will Satan gather together from the four quarters?
Revelation 20:5 *But the rest of the dead lived not again until the thousand years were finished.* (Here is the resurrection of damnation) Mat 5:29.

What is the ultimate fate of Satan and the wicked?
Revelation 20:9,10 *And they went up on the breadth of the earth, and compassed the camp of the saints about, and the beloved city: and fire came down from God out of heaven, and devoured them. And the devil that deceived them was cast into the lake of fire and brimstone where the beast and the false prophet are...*
Revelation 20:14,15 *And death and hell were cast into the lake of fire. This is the second death. And whosoever was not found written in the book of life was cast into the lake of fire.*
Malachi 4:1-3 *For, behold, the day cometh, that shall burn as an oven: and all the proud, yea, and all that do wickedly, shall be as stubble: and the day that cometh shall burn them up, saith the Lord of hosts, that it shall leave them neither root nor branch. But unto you that fear my name shall the sun of righteousness arise with healing in his wings; and ye shall go forth, and grow up as calves of the stall. And ye shall tread down the wicked: for they shall be ashes under the soles of your feet in the day that I shall do this, saith the Lord of hosts.*

How do those in heaven handle the loss of their loved ones who chose to perish in their pride and sin?
Revelation 21:4 *And God shall wipe away all tears from their eyes; and there shall be no more death, neither sorrow, nor crying, neither shall there be any more pain: for the former things are passed away.*

There you have it. No fancy translations, no magic, no smoke and mirrors, no ghosts, no purgatory, or ever burning hell. Very simply there will be only two groups: Those that know and love God and await that great day when they will be rewarded with new, immortal bodies, and those who have chosen to deny Him.

Chapter 23

When Will This World End?

*N*aturally we all desire to know when the world as we know it will end. This really wasn't a big deal to me prior this journey. However, I now look forward to that day even though there may be much sorrow to witness between now and then. Like we have seen, some will be elated when the second coming of Jesus brings their change from mortality to that of immortality. But sadly, many will not experience that same joy. So when will Jesus return? And what will that day actually be like?

For centuries, people of earth have a speculated about when the second coming would occur. And although many, often sincere, people have set dates in hopeful anticipation of Christ's return, all have been disappointed. In fact, this has happened so often that some have even wondered if Jesus will ever return. Yes, even the Bible records the words of those who question if this will ever happen.

> 2 Peter 3:3,4 *Knowing this first, that there shall come in the last days scoffers, walking after their own lust, and saying, where is the promise of thy coming? For*

since the fathers fell asleep, all things continue as they were from the beginning of the creation.

Yes, both believers and unbelievers alike wonder when Jesus will come back. And we can read in the book of Matthew of the disciples inquiring about this great event.

Matthew 24:3 *And as he sat upon the mount of Olives, the disciples came unto him privately, saying, Tell us, when shall these things be? And what shall be the sign of thy coming, and the end of the world?*

Jesus had been discussing future events with His followers in this particular chapter and they were basically asking him two questions. What were the events that would lead up to this great event, and secondly, when would He come again. Jesus would answer the question regarding the events leading up to His coming as we will see in a little bit. However, He did not tell them exactly when He would come back. Why? This is because He did not know the exact time of His return.

Mark 13:32 *But of that day and that hour knoweth no man, no not the angels which are in heaven, neither the Son, but the Father.*

You might wonder why Jesus, the Son of God, would not know when He would return to redeem His bride. But this is answered quite simply by understanding the pure submissive relationship that Jesus had with His Father. You see, Jesus gave everything for what the Bible calls the Bride of Christ, or in other words, His Church. A thorough study of the Jewish custom of preparing a dwelling place which must meet the Father's approval prior to a marriage and wedding feast will show the beauty of what Christ was implying in this passage.

John 14:2,3 *In my Father's house are many mansions: if it were not so, I would have told you. I go to prepare a place for you. And if I go and prepare a place for you, I will come again, and receive you unto myself, that where I am, there ye may be also.*

I am reminded again by reading this passage that what Jesus clearly stated proves that He must come back to receive us. Obviously, there is absolutely no reason to do this, nor anything else for that matter, if we go directly to heaven upon death. No, He has to come back "to receive" us.

So what about the questions His disciples asked on the Mount of Olives? What are the signs that can show us when His coming is near? Matthew twenty-four gives a very descriptive list of what Jesus told us to watch for.

Matthew 24:4-8 *And Jesus answered and said unto them, Take heed that no man deceive you. For many shall come in my name, saying, I am Christ; and shall deceive many. And ye shall hear of wars and rumours of wars: see that ye be not troubled: for all these things must come to pass, but the end is not yet. For nation shall rise against nation, and kingdom against kingdom: and there shall be famines, and pestilences, and earthquakes, in divers places. All of these are the beginnings of sorrows.*

Jesus goes on to state in verse fourteen that when the gospel is preached in all nations, then the end shall come. The gospel of course, is said to mean good news. I believe that good new is basically what I have learned on this journey: That Jesus died for my death! And because He loves us enough to pay that debt for us, He also loves us enough to give these warnings in Matthew.

> Matthew 24:21-27 *For then shall be great tribulation, such as was not since the beginning of the world to this time, no, nor ever shall be. And except those days should be shortened, there should no flesh be saved: but for the elect's sake those days shall be shortened. Then if any man shall say unto you, Lo, here is Christ, or there; believe it not. For there shall arise false Christs, and false prophets, and shall shew great signs and wonders; insomuch that, if it were possible, they shall deceive the very elect. Behold, I have told you before. Wherefore, if they shall say unto you, Behold, he is in the desert; go not forth: behold, he is in the secret chambers; believe it not.*

Why does Jesus give this warning about how He will come? Because He doesn't want anyone to think His coming will be a secret.

> Matthew 24:27 *For as the lightning cometh out of the east, and shineth even unto the west; so shall also the coming of the Son of man be.*

> Verse 30... *And then shall appear the sign of the Son of man in heaven: and then shall all the tribes of the earth mourn, and they shall see the Son of man coming in the clouds of heaven with power and great glory.*

The second coming of Jesus will not be a secret, but it will be a surprise to some.

> Matthew 24:37-39 *But as the days of Noe were, so shall also the coming of the Son of man be. For as in the days that were before the flood they were eating and drinking, marrying and giving in marriage, until*

the day that Noe entered the ark, And knew not until the flood came, and took them all away; so shall also the coming of the Son of man be.

Revelation 1:7 *Behold, he cometh with clouds; and every eye shall see him, and they also which pierced him: and all kindreds of the earth shall wail because of him. Even so, amen.*

During the time leading up until that great day evil will continue to contaminate the world. This is why Jesus spoke of a time of tribulation like the world has never experienced. And unfortunately, some people who put their trust in Christ will die for their faith. But those that are faithful to the end will ultimately have their place in His kingdom when they are resurrected unto immortality at His coming. These will be the ones who had put their total trust in the One whose sacrifice saved them from the second, or final, death.

Revelation 20:6 *Blessed and holy is he that hath part in the first resurrection: on such the second death hath no power, but they shall be priests of God and of Christ, and shall reign with him a thousand years.*

Even during the time when God's protective hand is removed from the earth and plagues are allowed to inflict the wicked prior to the coming of Jesus, those covered by His righteousness will be protected. God knows the ones who will ultimately choose to follow Him. And He will protect and provide for them until the end. This is just another reason why I could not deny God's love for me. Not only has He created me, provided for me, died for me, warned me and promised to protect me, but he has also given me the assurance of eternal life. Oh, and who can even imagine what He has planned for me in heaven and the new earth.

But if all the above isn't enough just think about what that great resurrection day will be like. What a great reunion there will be when those who have waited unconsciously in their graves are raised with new immortal bodies to meet the Lord in the air. All those moms and dads, grandmas and grandpas, sisters and brothers, and those little babies will be brought forth out of their graves in this most miraculous of events. And then those which are alive at the time of His coming will be caught up together to be with them all in the air.

What a day that will be, friend. And I hope and pray that you will be on the side of those who long for His coming. You see, our hearts must be right before that time. Prior to that day, every person's name will come before the judgment seat of Christ. And at the time when Jesus returns, all will have been decided. All destinies will be sealed. The judgment will be set and Jesus will return to execute that judgment.

> Revelation 22:11,12 *He that is unjust, let him be unjust still: and he which is filthy, let him be filthy still: and he that is righteous, let him be righteous still: and he that is holy, let him be holy still. And behold, I come quickly; and my reward is with me, to give every man according as his work shall be.*

Will your works be deemed worthy of a heavenly reward? I ask this because with all that we have learned, and with all that we see in the world today, there should be no questions that the stage is set for Jesus to return very soon!

Chapter 24

What Must I Do to be Saved?

As you know by now, this has been quite a ride. Starting with personal loss and a hunger for understanding what happens to a person when they die through formal and personal Bible studies, Karen and I have learned more than I ever thought possible. Not only were our eyes opened by the truth about those who have died, but we also learned other amazing facts as well. We learned about the character of God, the ministry of Jesus as well as the work of the Holy Spirit. In addition, I was particularly enlightened in learning about the purpose of God giving us the Ten Commandments and their role in the judgment of the world. And I will never forget studying the prophecies in the books of Matthew, Daniel and Revelation that clearly showed what will happen in the future. This proved to me once again that God must love us an awful lot because He tells us what's ahead.

Although it took some time because of my reluctance at first, God was patient with me and knew just what I needed. Then after absorbing everything this little brain of mine could hold, I came to a decision. God had done so much for me that I just had no choice but to repent of my selfish ways and ask Him to come into my heart. Then on June 7, 1990 in a small town in Michigan, Karen and I were baptized and I can honestly say that I have never regretted that decision.

Looking back at this experience has really got me thinking that just maybe we have got this religion stuff backwards. I mean, many of us go from church to church in hopes that we will learn the truth, or that just enough righteousness will rub off on us. But, doesn't it make more sense to learn what the Bible really teaches and then find a church that honors those teachings? Sure, it's easy for me to say that now. But I really do think my parents did me a favor by not forcing me into any particular tradition or religious direction when I was young. Whether by design or not, I'm happy for the way things turned out.

Am I perfect now? No way. Is God still working on me as I continue to study? Absolutely. Will I ever be perfect? That's something that I don't have to worry about because Jesus is and He took my death upon himself. Why did He do that for me? Because He knew that without His sacrifice there would have been no hope for me to have eternal life. You see, when Jesus died He reclaimed the power over death from that Satan had held for so long.

> **Hebrews 2:14,15** *Forasmuch then as the children are partakers of flesh and blood, he also himself likewise took part of the same; that through death he might destroy him that had the power of death, that is, the devil. <u>And deliver them who through fear of death were all their lifetime subject to bondage.</u>*

So why was I baptized after learning all this? Let me explain. Honestly, no one had ever told me what baptism was all about until that time. What I learned was that baptism is an outward profession of an inward change that occurs in the heart of a person. This inward change is what Jesus spoke about in his conversation with Nicodemus when He said you must be born again to inherit the kingdom. John 3:3. Therefore, sincere people who recognized their sinful nature and their need for a Savior can simply ask God to forgive them. Why is God willing to forgive us? Because of what Jesus had done for you and me on the cross. Yes, Jesus was the bridge builder sent by the Father to die in our place. And by overcoming His death, He overcame ours.

The Bible tells us that without the shedding of blood there is no remission of sins. Hebrews 9:22. Because God loves us and knows that sin separates us from Him, He provided a way in the form of His son Jesus. You see Jesus was the perfect sacrifice because He was sinless. He was perfectly obedient to the Father's will. This made His sacrifice sufficient for all who will accept Him.

Acts 4:12 *Neither is there salvation in any other: for there is none other name under heaven given among men, whereby we must be saved.*

Like I mentioned above, I never really thought baptism was all that important. But my view has changed, especially in light of what we have been discussing in the book. Even though we all would agree that death is bad, if there is such a thing as a good death it would be the death of self. Our sinful and selfish natures need to be put to death so we can experience newness of life! Without experiencing this change we can have little hope of true peace in this life, or eternal life to come. In other words, unless a person goes through this conversion process, he or she will not be given the gift of immortality otherwise known as eternal life. To put it yet another way… <u>for us to be changed when Jesus comes, we must be changed before He comes.</u>

Questioning Death

There is a story of an Ethiopian man in the Bible who had a desire to learn more about God. In much the same way that I learned about Jesus, this man was guided to the truth and touch by what he had learned. Almost immediately, this man wanted to do something about his new-found faith.

Acts 8:26-38 And the angel of the Lord spake unto Philip, saying, Arise, and go toward the south unto the way that goeth down from Jerusalem unto Gaza, which is desert. And he arose and went: and, behold, a man of Ethiopia, an eunuch of great authority under Candace queen of the Ethiopians, who had the charge of all her treasure, and had come to Jerusalem for to worship, Was returning, and sitting in his chariot read Esaias the prophet. Then the Spirit said unto Philip, Go near, and join thyself to this chariot. And Philip ran thither to him, and heard him read the prophet Esaias, and said, Understandest thou what thou readest? And he said, How can I, except some man should guide me? And he desired Philip that he would come up and sit with him. The place of the scripture which he read was this, He was led as a sheep to the slaughter; and like a lamb dumb before his shearer, so opened he not his mouth: In his humiliation his judgment was taken away: and who shall declare his generation? for his life is taken from the earth. And the eunuch answered Philip, and said, I pray thee, of whom speaketh the prophet this? of himself, or of some other man? Then Philip opened his mouth, and began at the same scripture, and preached unto him Jesus. And as they went on their way, they came unto a certain water: and the eunuch said, See, here is water; what doth hinder me to be baptized? And Philip said, If thou believest with all thine heart, thou mayest. And he answered and said, I believe that Jesus Christ is the Son of God. And he commanded the chariot to stand still: and they went down both into the water, both Philip and the eunuch; and he baptized him.

Another bonus to being baptized is the gift of the Holy Spirit that God gives to those who have truly repented and died to self. This is something I wanted and needed. You see, the Bible tells us that the Holy Spirit, or Comforter, is given to guide us into all truth. I thought this was a pretty cool deal since I had basically been without for most of my life. And just like eternal life, it was free! It's free to anyone who recognizes their inherited hopelessness and desires to know God better. Yes, God's Holy Spirit not only leads us into truth, but continues to guide us into ALL truth. After what I had learned, how could I refuse an offer like that?

Dear friend, maybe you have learned something new from reading this little book. If so, it's okay to admit it. Maybe you've learned many things that you never knew before and you feel sorry that a relationship with God has not been a priority in your life. But that's okay. There's no time like the present and He is waiting for you with open arms. The best news is, the process of coming home is a simple one. All we have to do is follow these steps.

1. Be taught to the point of understanding the issues.
2. Recognize that we are all sinners as revealed by looking into the mirror, or God's law.
3. Repent and forsake your sins.
4. Ask God to forgive you and thank Him for His grace.
5. Accept the blood of Jesus as sufficient for redeeming you.
6. Allow the old self to be put to death.
7. Accept the new start and the free gift of eternal life.
8. Ask for the Holy Spirit to guide you and work in your heart.

After learning much of what I have shared in this book, I had no choice but to follow the above steps including being baptized. The old selfish and sinful man needed to die and be raised again in newness of life. By now, I am hoping that the presentation of my journey has had at least some impact on your thinking.

Like many others today, I too was baptized, or christened, as an infant. And I believe my parents really thought they were doing the right thing. But you know, I was never taught anything prior to that event. Therefore, it really wasn't my decision. Looking back, I think that infant baptism is supposed to be some sort of a hurry-up claim of protection designed to keep the devil away. But could this practice actually give people a false sense of what it really means to be a Christian? And does the act really protect anyone? Now that I know what baptism really means, I wonder.

Maybe you were baptized as an infant as well. If so, your parents must have loved you an awful lot to have dedicated you to God. But like me, now you have made a new commitment to really accept Jesus for yourself. Maybe you have come to see God in a new light. Maybe you have even learned things that have moved you to make a new commitment to Bible study. If anything of the kind has happened in your life, simply follow the steps above and you are on your way. If not, that's alright too. Sometimes absorbing new information throws us off our horse for a little while. But hang in there friend. Don't let the devil discourage you. Simply ask God for strength and wisdom and He will give you just the help you need.

I didn't always believe in prayer but I definitely do now. In fact I will pray that this little book reaches you! And in that prayer I will ask the Father to send His Holy Spirit to be with you, guide you, and protect you as you step out on your own personal journey. I will pray that God will send someone across your path to help get you started and encourage you along the way. But you have a part to play in all of this too. Just have a desire in your heart to know the Father better. If you will do that, I believe He will do the rest.

When this all started I was just an ordinary person with questions about death. Like many of you I experienced loss, anger, wonder and doubt. I felt very small and insignificant in the whole scheme of things and did not know if I had any purpose whatsoever. I spent time, money and brain cells in attempts to fill the void in my heart and numb the pain. And I know that many others have holes in their hearts as well, especially if they have lost loved ones. For me, learning about God and His love for mankind filled the void many times over. And I hope my story can help in leading you to the source of healing.

Dear friend, by now you must know that the devil did not want you to read this little book. But this is exactly why I wrote it. I hate what the devil has done to this world and I simply could not rest easy keeping all this to myself. Maybe you could call it the Holy Spirit's work or maybe you could say that this guy just had to get this stuff off his chest to make himself feel better. There might even be those who would suggest that I have some sort of vendetta to carry out against the church. People can think and say what they want to. Honestly, I believe that God wants us all to share what we know about Him. He wants us to tell His children that He loves them. And He needs many more messengers.

As I close this book I would just ask you to open your eyes. Look around at the world today. If you see the confusion, if you see deception, if you see pain and suffering, if you see death and sorrow, ask yourself who has caused all this mess. You know what I believe. The more the devil works to deceive the people of earth, the farther they will be from the love, blessings, and protection of our loving Father. God will provide peace in times of trouble for those who know and love Him. Remember that God came down to earth in the form of His Son, holding His arms wide open for you and for me. Also, the Bible tells us that God has commanded His angels to hold back the winds of strife just a little longer so that every person has had their chance to learn the issues and make a decision. But soon, and very soon, God will have seen enough. He will send His Son to receive His Bride, execute His judgment upon the rebellious, and purify the earth. Are you ready?

Dear friend, I almost hate to say this but things on earth are going to get much, much worse before they get better. We are all going to need something to hang on to. Rather than grasping for empty promises and mysterious superstitions, please give your Heavenly Father a chance. Get to know Him. He is waiting to embrace you just like any loving Father would embrace their lost child after years of watching them go through many struggles, pains and sorrows. He really loves you!

Dear Father,

Sometimes I do not feel worthy to come to you because I know I can never return the love you have shown to me. Forgive me, Father, for the time I have wasted pursuing my own selfish desires instead of serving you. Today I have made a decision. I have decided to take my will from the hands of the devil and turn it over to you. I know now that Jesus died for me because He wants me to be in heaven with you. And I also know that the devil wants me to be destroyed with him.

Father, I am no longer going to believe that I can live forever apart from your free gift, and my desire is to share this with as many people as I can. Please forgive me for all the sins I have committed in the past and help me not to sin in the future. I am accepting the blood of your Son to cleanse me, and because I now understand why Jesus gave Himself for me, I no longer want to hurt Him. Anyone who is willing to die for my death deserves much more than I can ever give. But I sure want to try. Thank you for all that you have done for me and even though I may go through many difficult trials as a result of standing for the truth, I know you will never leave me, nor forsake me. Thanks for everything.

Love, Your Child

P.S. Whether I am asleep in the grave, or alive and remaining faithful when Jesus returns, I can hardly wait to put on the gift of immortality and see you in heaven, face to face.

Have you ever wondered what really happens to a person when they die? Here's a true story of how one man's journey into this mysterious question revealed many surprising answers.

Contact Info

For more information or to order more copies please visit…

www.QuestioningDeath.com